Ned Kissinger's

The
Battlefield
of Retirement

Stories and Strategies from the Front Lines

Edited by Eric N. Seaborg & Margaret S. Kiewitt

Outskirts Press, Inc.
Denver, Colorado

Ned Kissinger's The Battlefield of Retirement
Stories and Strategies from the Front Lines
All Rights Reserved
Copyright © 2007 Ned Kissinger, CFP®, ChFEBC
V2.0 R 1.0

Outskirts Press
http://www.outskirtspress.com

Paperback ISBN: 978-1-4327-0437-7
Hardback ISBN: 978-1-4327-0708-8

Outskirts Press and the "OP" logo are trademarks belonging to Outskirts Press, Inc.

Printed in the United States of America

ACKNOWLEDGMENTS

I wanted to take a moment to thank those who were so instrumental in bringing this book to fruition.

To Eric Seaborg and Maggie Kiewitt from Aspect Associates: without you this book would never have happened. Thank you for the two hours every Sunday afternoon at Panera Bread for months on end. Your ideas, input, and work truly are the reason this book is now published. I can't thank you enough; the world would be a better place if more people were like you.

To my wife and daughter: every morning I wake up with the sense that I am blessed beyond belief. Why shouldn't I feel that way? I have the two most beautiful women in the world, who love and support me. Thank you for letting me chase after my dreams and work all those long hours. Since you support me the way you do, those dreams are our dreams. Every success I have in life is our success. Our lives are knit together by God. Thank you for loving me.

To my parents, Bill and Debbie Kissinger: through your love and guidance you have provided me with the tools and work ethic to complete this project. Thank you for building this great financial planning business and allowing me to be a part of it. When I was young I used to dream about being a sports legend or some famous person, but now my hope is to be like you one day.

To my sister Maggi: while we don't see each other that often, the support you gave me when I was young has helped mold me into the person I am today. You are a dynamic and successful businesswoman, and I am truly blessed to call you not only my sister, but my friend.

To Aaron: I never got to say good-bye to you. Our friendship and the effect you had on my life lives on even in your death. I miss you.

To Pastor Paul: your testimony through the dark and hard times has taught me that giving up is not an option. Keep running the race.

And finally I would like to thank God. Thank you for blessing my life with two beautiful women, great friends, great parents, a great job, a great country, and great in-laws. I could go on and on and never be able to thank you enough for the blessings of this life. Even though this book was not for me to preach the gospel, I pray that everyone would get to know you. You are a merciful and gracious God. You forgive and forget our mistakes. Thank you for seeking me out and showing me your loving and forgiving heart. The best decision I ever made was to follow you.

Proverbs 3:5-6 "Trust in the Lord with all your heart and lean not on your own understanding; in all ways acknowledge Him, and he will make your paths straight."

TABLE OF CONTENTS

A NOTE FROM THE EDITORS

In the summer of 2006 we were honored by Ned Kissinger, who wanted us to help him with this informative book. It began a journey that would expose us to a wealth of information from a brilliant and energetic mind; an up-and-coming leader in the financial management industry. More importantly, the process allowed us the insight into Ned, the person.

In a business where financial planners are plentiful, Ned has a bedside manner that is kind and sincere to complement his knowledge. The months working with him constructing this book revealed an individual who was mature beyond his years. He is a pioneer of sorts who has the magic to blend traditional values with contemporary approaches as penned in this user-friendly book.

What was clear from the conception of this project was Ned's vision to publish a guide that would help the reader prepare for retirement. Assuming that most individuals have built a nest egg for the future, his passion in discussing the most effective ways to collect and cultivate those funds is the focus of his writing. To illustrate this, he sprinkles numerous real-life stories throughout the book to emphasize his points. Because he attended Gettysburg College in Pennsylvania, he wanted to associate the decision-making strategies utilized during the famous Battle for Gettysburg into this entertaining financial account.

When Kissinger Financial Services became a part of Sanders Morris Harris Inc., Ned found himself partnered with his mentor, his dad. Before electing to team with SMH

Capital Inc., William ("Bill") Kissinger had built his company into a successful, strong operation while maintaining a family-oriented atmosphere. Bill's legacy of working effectively, one-on-one with each client has served as a role model for Ned. This special father/son relationship strengthens the business through an entrepreneurial spirit that Ned possesses.

We know you will enjoy and learn from this book as Ned takes you through a step-by-step journey to that retirement pot of gold.

Margaret S. Kiewitt
Eric N. Seaborg
Aspect Associates, LLC
www.aspectassociates.com

PROLOGUE

I was twenty-two years old and just a few months from graduating from Gettysburg College. I hadn't decided what I wanted to be when I "grew up," but I figured something would come along to interest me.

One afternoon in early spring, I had just finished a round of golf at a local course and met up with my girlfriend (future wife) at the Lincoln Diner for a bite. This was a popular eatery where you could get a good, quick meal on a student budget. The place began to fill up as we waited and waited for our waitress to make an appearance. I grew impatient and in an uncharacteristic manner for me, I approached the manager to complain. Without hesitating, he pointed to a uniformed woman attempting to balance a food tray and said, "There's your waitress," as he walked away. Hunching down in the corner of the busy restaurant, a frail, elderly woman with a pasty complexion was straining to lift the platters of food that dwarfed her meager frame.

When she finally made her way to our table and apologized for the delay, I became curious about her. Why was she here working in this diner at her age? I had come to know the Lincoln Diner as a place where eighteen-year-olds have trouble keeping up with the pace, much less a woman of her age and frailty. We struck up a conversation, and I soon learned that the object of my attention was in her early 80s. My inquiring mind wanted to know more because she seemed to struggle with the physical responsibilities of the job. My gut told me it wasn't the type of career that a woman of her capabilities would choose voluntarily. Unfortunately, my intuition was correct. I discovered that not long ago she became a widow and was forced to find a job for the first time in her life. Apparently, upon the death of her husband, she learned that he had chosen something called a no survivor option on his pension plan payout. Like many in this country, she could not survive on Social Security alone. She wasn't physically or physiologically equipped for the job she was doing, but she had no choice but to do the job anyway.

It was at that moment, on that day, this sad story changed my life. I realized that I was looking into the face of poverty; she did not have the years or the strength left to change her life for the better. I made the conscious decision to become a financial planner and specialize in helping America prepare for a secure retirement. I have been blessed to have had the opportunity to make this dream come true. Helping people prepare for the golden years has given me many moments of euphoria and many moments of sadness. It is my ongoing commitment, my family, who lovingly supports me, and the nameless frail lady of the Lincoln Diner, who gave me a gift through her sacrifice, that compel me to reach out to others through this book.

In many ways, preparing for retirement resembles a series of battle strategies not so different from those faced by wartime generals. Since my career epiphany occurred at Gettysburg, I believe it is fitting that I use that famous Civil War battlefield as the backdrop for this book.

No two stories are alike, and throughout the book you will travel with me as I recount some of my experiences working with the "soldiers" as they prepared for retirement. This map of the battlefield will help direct a course of action toward retirement to enable you to enjoy one of the most precious periods of life. So join me on the battlefield of retirement as we prepare strategies to lead you to a victory of comfortable living.

CHAPTER 1
DEFINING YOUR CAMPAIGN FOR RETIREMENT

"Don't simply retire from something; have something to retire to."

HARRY EMERSON FOSDICK

In the summer of 1863, General Robert E. Lee was determined to take the Civil War to the North to draw the fighting away from Virginia. He sought an opportunity to forage for food and supplies from the rich farmlands of Pennsylvania. On July 1st, the Confederacy marched down the Chambersburg Pike toward the small Pennsylvania town of Gettysburg. Beyond Lee's immediate task of defeating the enemy was a cause to bring a better life for those he was leading in battle. You, on the other hand, march into the working world to embark on a journey that millions have taken before you. Planning your retirement is the path to a better life and the opportunity to build your future. General Lee's need to prepare for combat is similar to your need to prepare for retirement. He needed to win a battle to ultimately win a war by preparing a solid strategy. Like Lee, you need a plan to be victorious in retirement. Hopefully, your employer has provided a retirement program to build a foundation for your golden years. Using a little discipline, you can amass a monetary war chest that can withstand unpredictable life changes while constructing a comfortable nest egg, and your outcome can be very different from that of the Confederacy.

For most of us, saving for a rainy day was engrained in

1

us by our parents. Savings accounts, retirement plans, and tax laws have all promoted this concept. If you hide your money in the employer's bunker, you will be able to find that money later in life when you need it. If you have invested wisely, you will have received interest and appreciation on your original savings. There are many bunkers from which to choose, and this book will help you determine which is right for you. But, first, you have an equally important retirement decision to make.

Just as you decided what you wanted to be when you grew up, now you must decide where you want to be and what you want to do when you are retired. Why is this just as important as a financial plan for retirement? If you define your perfect retirement as growing tomatoes and selling them from a produce stand in your front yard, it is likely to take less annual income than if you plan to take two cruises each year. You have many options for retirement activities these days because most of us are living longer, healthier lives.

According to the Center for Disease Control (CDC), our life expectancy is inching upward. The CDC analyzed over 97 percent of all state death certificates issued in 2001 and found for men, life expectancy increased from 74.3 years in 2000 to 74.4 years in 2001. Women kept pace with an increase from 79.7 years to 79.8 years for the same period. A small advance in the percentage may not impact your thinking. However, the constant war being waged by medicine to prolong life expectancy over the years is a true indicator of our desire to have a better and longer life. Such victorious battles against polio, smallpox, malaria, and other pandemics have demonstrated the constant aspiration to keep us healthy for as long as possible.

Knowing that the troops in the medical profession are working harder to prolong our lives, once you retire from the workforce there will be plenty of quality time to fill. Ask yourself, do you want to continue to work full- or part-time? How about going back to school to get that degree you always wished you had, or take dance lessons, or travel? Want to visit your grandchildren more frequently, stop cooking and eat out every night, play more golf, or perhaps volunteer?

Similarly, you have many options concerning where you want to live during retirement. Do you want to remain in your current house? Downsize and buy a small place? Rent an apartment? Move to a retirement village or an over-55 housing development? Buy a mobile home? Buy a vacation home or move in with family?

It is not as simple as just saving for tomorrow. You must embrace the strategy that General Lee needed to envision winning the Civil War. He had to prepare for the battles ahead. You also have to prepare by knowing what you want to do and where you want to do it. Only then can you determine how much money it will take for you to live comfortably and achieve your retirement goals.

Let me illustrate this important concept with two "voices."

One elderly gentleman, who owned and operated his own successful company for many years, had amassed a sizeable retirement income. He and his wife spent winters in the warm south and went north for the cool breezes in the summer. After a very short time in retirement, the gentleman discovered that he did not have enough activities to fill his days during the winter. Although he had the capital to purchase a fleet of limousines, he went to work part-time for a limo service, shuffling travelers to and from the local airport. It wasn't because he needed the income—he needed a reason for getting up each day with someplace to go and something to do that

made him feel like a useful member of society.

Then there was the female client who had worked since she was fifteen years old and retired in her mid-sixties. She had done her financial homework and knew she had accumulated enough savings to allow her to live quite well during retirement. Within a few months of retiring, she ended up in the hospital with severe, debilitating back spasms. After undergoing a battery of expensive tests, the doctor couldn't find a medical reason for the painful spasms. While going over the test results with her, the physician discovered that she was struggling with retirement. She had never married, and therefore her identity was defined solely by the jobs she had occupied. She was like a woman without a country...no job, no identity. There was nothing to fill the endless free time that seemed to drag on each day. The more the woman talked about the situation, the more the doctor came to understand the stress she placed on herself attempting to battle the situation. His final medical diagnosis was stress-induced spasms. Had this client taken the time to define what retirement would be for her before she retired, she could have saved herself a lot of pain!

Our two warriors prepared themselves well for the financial battle, but failed to defend against the enemies of boredom and lack of self-worth upon retirement. Often, however, the signs of a troubled retirement are not so clear. Alcoholism, depression, and self-medication may be by-products of trying to battle retirement. An article in the *Journal of Studies on Alcohol* found that in the years 2000 and 2001, it was estimated that 11 million elderly Americans, or approximately one-third of the population, consumed alcohol. Another study estimated that the number of senior citizens in need of substance abuse treatment will rise from 1.7 million in 2001 to approximately 4.4 million by 2020. This is due in part to the aging of the baby boomers.

> **Learn from the client who failed to define what his retirement would be like.** He had had a very successful career in governmental services and had never used illegal drugs or abused alcohol. He was always on the go and possessed a clearly defined role of importance. A few months after he retired, he began to fall victim to substance abuse. His struggle found him fighting to find a reason to get up everyday.

A self-induced temporary euphoria is not a battle plan, but more a suicide mission where the likelihood of survival is dim. Perhaps it is a risk you are willing to take, but it isn't the one that your spouse, children, or friends would choose for you. General Lee wasn't just fighting for the "day," he was fighting for a future for those who would survive him.

Ever heard the old adage, "I married you for better or worse, but not for lunch everyday"? Marital stress may also be a result of poor retirement planning.

Not all of your activities in retirement have to be together, but if you are married, it is essential that the two of you discuss your goals and reach consensus. Just as Robert E. Lee had to collaborate with his other generals to build a strategy suitable for victory, couples must stand shoulder to shoulder during the defining process. A marriage may not last once a couple moves to Timbuktu if it isn't agreed upon before the move is carried out. Additionally, those arguments from early in the marriage about finances may double back and attack your flank if you don't agree on activities and items on which to spend retirement funds. Remember, one person doesn't know what is better for both if it's not discussed ahead of time. Besides, it seems a shame to have any hard-won retirement resources surrendered to the divorce attorneys.

Let me share a happy retirement story to illustrate how the time spent on defining your retirement can lead to success in the battle of retirement planning.

I know a man who had always wished he had taken the opportunity in his youth to study abroad and earn an advanced degree. He made this his first goal of retirement, setting up a financial strategy that enabled him to pay for his education, travel and living expenses while studying at Cambridge University in England. He persevered and earned his doctorate at the age of 76.

So with our objective to win the battle of a happy retirement, let us plan the strategy.

List on the left side of a piece of paper those activities you currently engage in that you'd like to continue in retirement. Next to that, list all of the new things you want to try or do once you are retired. In the third column, list the frequency with which you desire to do the activities listed in the first and second columns. Your worksheet may look something like this:

PRE-RETIREMENT INTEREST/HOBBY	POST-RETIREMENT INTEREST/HOBBY	HOW OFTEN
Playing Golf		2x WEEKLY
Visiting Grandkids	Volunteer	MONTHLY
	Vacation Travel	4x YEAR

Once you have defined your retirement via these desires, you can then begin to plan for how you will finance those activities. Don't forget, if you are married, these are "we" questions. Here are some ideas to give your thinking some focus.

- Do you want to expand on your education? This can be accomplished through continuing education, taking courses for credit at a local college, or by attending workshops and seminars. Keep in mind it costs much more to earn a degree than to take a series of continuing-education classes or participate in one-time learning sessions.

- What actions will you take to maintain a healthy lifestyle? Fitness classes, non-structured exercise such as walking or recreational sports? Walking is cheap; all you need is a good pair of shoes. Joining or continuing a membership in an athletic club or fitness center will cost retirement dollars.

- How much do you want to vacation or travel? Where do you want to go? Certain times of the year are more costly to travel.

- Will you start or continue a hobby? What expenses will be involved?

- Will you be eating out more or staying at home in the kitchen to cook?

- How about social adventures like going to museums, plays, movies, the library?

- Do you prefer to do your activities alone, with only your spouse, or with a group?

- Do you want to contribute and become active in spiritual or charitable organizations?

- Do you want to go back to work full- or part-time?

- Do you want to start your own business?

- Have you considered long-term care insurance to combat the gradual or sudden decline of your health?

- Where do you want to live?

- Will any member of your family be dependent upon you financially when you retire?

- Do you want to leave an estate?

Before the battle begins, you may wish to develop a strategy. You and your spouse will need to either compile this list together or make separate lists, which you will combine to define your retirement as a couple. For example, an activity you may wish to continue into retirement on a more routine basis is golf, while adding travel and perhaps joining a bridge club. More importantly, you'll want to define how often you'll take part in such activities. Before retirement you may golf every other Saturday, but once departed from the work world, you may up that activity to a few times a week. The same holds true for travel, where your time availability may allow for more trips to visit family, friends, or faraway places.

Naturally I cannot define the perfect retirement for you. Only you can do that. But if you take nothing else with you from reading this book, please understand and embrace the importance of defining your retirement for yourself.

CHAPTER 2
PROCRASTINATION IS YOUR ENEMY

"Suspect each moment, for it is a thief, tiptoeing away with more than it brings."

JOHN UPDIKE

Near the end of the first day of the Battle of Gettysburg, Confederate General Robert E. Lee ordered General R. S. Ewell to seize the high ground on Cemetery Ridge "if practicable." Lee felt his order was clear, and he expected Ewell to claim this valuable military real estate before the Union could. Like all good generals, Lee knew that a window of opportunity is opened and closed quickly in wartime. On the other hand, General Ewell, knowing that his troops were exhausted, elected to interpret Lee's term "if practicable" as reason to wait until the next day to allow his troops to rest before carrying out the order. Ewell put off the directive of his superior, believing that a moment of rest would not jeopardize the situation. Unfortunately, this afforded the Union the opportunity to dig in along Cemetery Ridge overnight and gain the high ground. Because of Ewell's procrastination, the South lost a critical advantage.

Ewell's downfall is the enemy within every one of us. An enemy so well disguised that it often creates more silent havoc than any tangible force within our lives. The destruction this silent enemy leaves in its wake is usually followed by expressions such as: "If only I had...," "Why didn't I...," and "How could I have been so blind?" This enemy is procrastination, and only you can combat this habit-forming foe.

Too often we tend to emulate General Ewell's hesitation when it comes to retirement planning. Why worry about something today when there is a lifetime of tomorrows? For some reason, we walk through life with a crystal-ball mentality, thinking that we can foresee our life expectancy, golden years, and health crises. We begin to convince ourselves that our crystal ball never fogs up with the uncertainties of life. We see natural progression points such as saving for tomorrow after the children are grown. When the coaching responsibilities, PTA, recitals, and college tuitions are over, and car, life, and homeowners insurance policies are paid up, then we can find time to plan retirement and perhaps work with a financial advisor. Suddenly, we arrive at retirement age and, like General Ewell, our procrastination has cost us our advantage.

Here's another way to look at it. Procrastination causes many of us to:

- **Put off paying the debt we've amassed falling victim to easily obtained credit loans.**

- **Put off defining how and where we want to live during our retirement.**

- **Delay taking full advantage of our employer's benefit plans and tax laws.**

- **Put off educating ourselves about personal finances and wise methods of investment.**

- **Put off creating a comprehensive financial plan and investing in the plan early and regularly.**

- Some even postpone thinking about and planning their estate.

Here's a voice from the battlefield that illustrates the dangers of procrastination.

A young husband and wife team made huge salaries in their early careers, but they spent every dime. They took lavish vacations several times each year; thought nothing of shelling out $200-$300 for dinner three or four times a week; drove luxury cars. In their early forties, they decided to start a family. With the arrival of the new troops, they purchased a large house and carried a $500,000 mortgage. Several crises occurred within the family, and the couple found themselves $82,000 in credit-card debt. Averaging the mortgage interest rate and the credit-card interest, they paid about $4,600 monthly in just interest payments, never managing to pay more than the minimum required amount. Still they sent their children to expensive colleges and racked up massive student loans. Now we have a couple in their early sixties, buried in debt with no retirement savings. If they were to retire, they would have only Social Security income, which won't cover the cost of their minimum monthly payments. They have no choice; this couple will work until they die.

At the opposite end of the battlefield, meet a teacher, a single mother of two. Since teachers, especially new ones, make modest salaries, this lady decided to live by the motto "If I don't have the cash, I don't buy it." In addition to her frugal lifestyle, starting in her first year of teaching, she contributed 10% of her salary to a tax-sheltered annuity. As her salary increased annually, the woman continued to live by her cash only rule and continued to contribute to her tax shelter. Of course, that 10% contribution grew annually with every raise. After a successful 35-year teaching career, this client retired with an income higher than her final annual income when she was teaching.

The lifestyle philosophies of these two clients are as different as the philosophies of the Union and the Confederacy. Lifestyle, not income, dictated each client's battle strategy. The teacher developed a plan that foiled procrastination, while the husband and wife embraced procrastination, living only for the day. At the war's end, the procrastinators were defeated; the saver victorious. If you haven't already decided which side you are on, today is the day.

Procrastination is only one of many roadblocks to avoid on your march toward a comfortable and pleasant retirement, but it is the deadliest. Here's the battle plan for attacking procrastination:

- **Do your research and find a good financial planner that shares your values and will focus on your needs. You need three top-notch professionals in your financial life: a financial planner, a CPA, and a lawyer. No one can do the work of all three.**

- **Create a picture of your current financial situation by developing a financial statement and a cash-flow statement.**

- **Assess your credit situation and make wise choices when using credit. Here's one of my favorite sayings to illustrate this point. "Overuse of plastic can be hazardous to your wealth."**

- **Eliminate debt that erodes your savings as soon as possible.**

- Set a goal for investing a portion of your income now. According to Albert Einstein, "The most powerful force in the universe is compound interest."
- Start saving and investing on a regular basis. In other words, pay yourself first. Consider this example and see how an initial investment of $50,000, with regular monthly contributions of $1,000, will grow. Ideally, with an average return of 10% your investment will grow to $3,252,357.89 in over thirty years. You may need to establish a smaller initial contribution and smaller monthly contributions, but the point is clear. The earlier you begin to coordinate contributions, the quicker your retirement account will grow.

OVER 30 YEARS
$50,000 INVESTMENT
$1,000 MONTHLY CONTRIBUTION

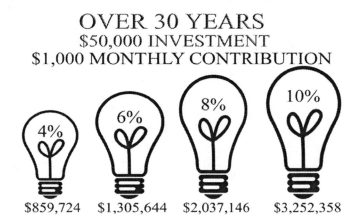

4%	6%	8%	10%
$859,724	$1,305,644	$2,037,146	$3,252,358

CHAPTER 3
CREDIT CAN BE A VERY LARGE CANNON

"The rich ruleth over the poor and the borrower is servant to the lender."

PROVERBS 22:7

On the afternoon of July 3, 1863, Confederate General James Longstreet ordered the largest cannonade ever heard on our continent at that time. This massive bombardment intended to soften the Union position prior to the now famous Pickett's Charge. Unfortunately, the cannons overshot their Union targets, landing harmlessly in the cornfields behind the enemy's position, and Pickett led the Confederates directly toward the Union army, who were unaffected by the Confederate bombardment.

Depending on how you utilize credit will determine its effectiveness. When thinking in terms of Longstreet's cannon bombardment, he was providing the artillery to achieve a goal, but he used it ineffectively. Like Longstreet, you can be provided the artillery to use credit to achieve your financial goals. But a misuse of credit will only worsen your situation. Therefore, to control credit and make it work to your advantage, you must understand the principles. There are three types of debt.

First, if an opportunity exists to make a financial gain over time and credit is needed to finance the deal, then it can be worthwhile. This advantageous debt works for you only if a strategy has been developed to manage and eventually pay off the debt.

Next, there are points in our lives where an unexpected situation arises and you need immediate cash to resolve the issue. Health problems or unforeseen home repairs may require instant attention to maintain your quality of life and keep the problem from worsening. This second type of debt we refer to as necessary debt because it involves a necessary outlay of money. Again, there should be a plan in place to pay down the debt and free yourself of a long-term financial burden.

Finally, the greatest monster is, of course, unnecessary debt. This is where the banks and credit card companies win the war. Their objective is to float attractive rates to the public that will entice the consumer to spend before s/he is ready. There is a simple way of determining if you fall victim to this strategy. If your credit is working for the bank, a credit card company, or other lender instead of for you (i.e. making minimum monthly payments with interest rates in double digits), it's missing your target. Let me tackle some of these issues in more detail.

In today's society, good credit is necessary, and one sometimes must purchase things on installment in order to establish a viable credit rating. A home mortgage is one example of advantageous debt. Few of us could ever afford the American dream of owning a home if we didn't take out a mortgage. However, aim too high by purchasing a home above your means, and your mortgage becomes a financial liability. Other examples of advantageous debt may include education or career training and borrowing money to start your own business. Although you may need student loans or other kinds of credit for either education or training or for establishing a new business, the premise is that you will make a higher income as a result, thus enabling you to eliminate this debt in a timely manner.

Although you will be paying interest on the credit or borrowed money, the benefits will far outweigh your expenditure down the road.

Necessary debt is usually unavoidable. Buying a car to ensure that you have reliable transportation to get to your job, and unexpected, uninsured medical debt are two examples of necessary debt. In these instances, you have no choice but to purchase the goods or services to resolve the issue. If you have to put those purchases on credit, so be it. Your "cannonade," however, should amount to a financial blitz that will enable you to pay off this monetary burden as quickly as possible to avoid accumulating a large amount of interest debt on top of the original loan.

And then there is the most cruel enemy of all, unnecessary debt. Examples include putting nonessential, luxury items on a credit card: maybe a cruise, expensive dinners, furs, jewelry, etc. Revisit the couple whose voices we heard in Chapter Two, the ones who made plenty of money, but spent every dime and then some. Listen carefully when they tell you that they amassed $82,000 in unnecessary debt and will be working the rest of their lives to eliminate that debt. Wiser to heed the voice of the teacher who lived by "if I can't pay cash for it now, I don't buy it now." Credit can be an ally or an enemy, depending on how well you manage your debt.

Credit lessons should begin early in life; even children should be taught that the habitual need for instant gratification can lead to a lifelong battle with creditors. Let me share my own story to illustrate.

When I was a teenager, my father gave me a credit card with a $250 limit, knowing that I should be able to pay off this amount monthly on my odd jobs salary. Dad wanted me to know how important it was to establish an

excellent credit rating as soon as possible, and he wanted to make certain that I had the opportunity to learn to manage my credit obligations. Then Dad took it one step further. He made a sticker that was adhered to my credit card, just under my signature. The sticker read, "Warning! Overuse of this card can be hazardous to your wealth." I learned my lesson well and am forever grateful to Dad for this early example. In fact, it worked so well that in about sixteen years, I'll use it with my own daughter!

And then there is this story about living for the day and ignoring the future:

This couple had a moderate but comfortable income with one Achilles heel; the inability to say "no." They preferred a lifestyle of spending without consideration of the unexpected. For years, this lifestyle enabled them to keep up with the bills without overextending. Fortunately, their children grew up without creating a financial burden and ventured from home leaving them in a relatively good position. Despite the vibrant health of both, the breadwinner of the family (the husband) elected to retire at age 65 and live the good life. For a time, it appeared that living for the day was going to pay off for our couple. They had enjoyed luxury vacations, new cars every few years, and the ability to buy when the feeling hit them. What they didn't expect was the return to the nest of an adult child, but things still appeared to be manageable. Unfortunately, the adult child, who worked sporadically and didn't contribute to the household finances, never left the roost. Soon he married and had children of his own, which our elderly couple now had to support. Sadly, this lifestyle was the worst possible scenario for a couple who never had a keen eye for budgeting. Over time, credit cards were being used to pay credit cards, and the little bit of retirement and cash was depleted. When the adult child was forced to leave home because of the dire straights he helped create, an older sibling took over the parents' finances. She sold their home to pay off a second mortgage and soon after filed for bankruptcy to get them out from under unmanageable credit card debt. She also managed to find an affordable retirement community for them while handling their banking. Although the couple was blessed to have such a strong and caring daughter, they have expensive health insurance and no estate, not even enough for a modest burial. Social Security maintains their month-to-month financial stability, and they hope another crisis will not surface. Heed the battle story of this couple who lost their home, their freewheeling independence, and to some extent their dignity to unnecessary credit foes and the seduction of credit. Fortunately, the love and determination of the daughter, who was willing to work so hard to correct her parents' credit mistakes, has kept this story one step away from a tragedy.

And finally...

A six-figure-income businessman lost his job at age 62 due to a hostile takeover. Although this man had practiced a lifetime of wise credit decisions, he could not bear to tell his wife that they could no longer afford to maintain their current lifestyle. He began to charge everyday goods and services such as gas, groceries, and dry cleaning bills. When he maxed out one credit card, he'd open another, take advantage of low interest to transfer the balance from the first, and continue on his "merry" way. No one suspected the depth of his credit woes until he died suddenly. The wife then began to receive myriad overdue credit card statements and had no better means to resolve this debt than her husband had. Added to her financial despair was an enormous sense of guilt. Had she known or even suspected how her husband was struggling with the finances, she would have gladly used her own income to pay household bills and to maintain a more restrained lifestyle. In the case of this couple, the wife had never handled any of the finances, paid any bills, etc., so she had no reason to be leery of her husband's claim that he was handling all of their expenses with his unemployment check and savings. She also knew he loathed credit cards and refused to use them for anything other than an emergency. How sad it was that this battle-weary warrior transferred his financial burden to his wife, who now had to struggle on alone. What began simply as necessary debt quickly turned to unnecessary debt with over usage. Our businessman failed to confide in his spouse and together plan a strategy. Like Pickett, he charged straight across that open field and faced a barrage from his creditors that will long haunt his survivors.

Hopefully you now have a solid understanding of the enemy we face in mismanaging credit. So here's a battle strategy for using credit wisely.

Resolve to use credit only when it is to your advantage and/or absolutely necessary. Do not use credit for everyday goods and services or for unnecessary luxury items.

- **Stay on top of your credit rating. Take advantage of one or all of the companies who offer either free or for-a-minimal-fee credit reports. Know your credit score. The better your credit rating or score, the easier it is for you to obtain necessary credit at a lower rate. You can either call or use the Web to obtain your credit report from one of these reputable organizations.**

- Experian   1-888-397-3742 www.experian.com
- Equifax   1-800-685-1111 www.equifax.com
- Trans Union   1-800-888-4213 www.tuc.com

- Develop a family plan for tapping into your credit. If you are married, you and your spouse should decide jointly when it is appropriate to use credit and when it is appropriate to wait until you can pay for your purchase in cash. Both spouses should always have full knowledge and understanding of the status of the family debt.

- Limit the number of credit cards you have and use. Is it necessary to have a gas credit card and department store credit cards, or is it sufficient to have a widely accepted card like Visa, MasterCard, or Discover Card to utilize for necessary credit? As a rule, the more cards you carry in your pocket, the easier it is to run up excessive debt. In military terms, it's the old divide and conquer. You are less likely to be fully aware of the amount needed to pay off a number of different cards than if you use only one.

- Pay off the entire balance on the credit card every month. If you don't, you will notice that your credit card company will "reward" you by increasing your spending limit. Don't think this is because the company loves you and wants you to have more money to spend. Credit card companies adore customers who pay only the minimum payment month after month. Just as compound interest is a wonderful thing for you when you are saving, compound interest becomes a dangerous weapon used against you when you are charging. Add a pair of roller blades to your current high-balance, high-interest credit card, pay only the minimum payment, and, my friend, you will still be paying for these roller blades long after you are too old to use them!

- Put my dad's sticker on your credit card. Believe me, it will serve as a constant reminder to rethink every purchase and decide if it is a necessary one.

But, you may say that this warning has come too late. Maybe you already have bad credit. So what can you do now? Try this battle strategy for eliminating unnecessary or bad debt.

- The first step toward eliminating this debt is to analyze how you got into this situation. Like Gettysburg, every major battle begins with a small encounter. You must meet this enemy head on and resolve that, once defeated; you may never skirmish with it again.

- As a family, develop a plan to attack the debt immediately. If you need the help of a credit counselor, get it now.

- Resolve to close all nonessential credit accounts and to use the remaining account(s) only in case of emergency. In other words, develop new, wiser credit strategies.

- Research using a home equity loan to eliminate your bad debt. But be aware that this is not the "ultimate weapon." You must be certain that you are able to pay the higher monthly mortgage payment or risk losing your home. And remember that there are some costs involved in refinancing. Some states have higher rates than others do.

- Seek to consolidate your debt at the lowest possible

interest. Don't shy away from contacting your creditors to negotiate lower rates. They would rather collect on most of the debt than collect nothing if you were to declare bankruptcy.

- Pay monthly as much as possible on the highest interest debt. When you have eliminated this debt, attack the next highest interest debt.

- Once you have eliminated all of your bad debt, do not charge more on any credit account than you can afford to pay off at the end of the month.

As a summary, let's return to our analogy between credit and the cannonade. Had Longstreet's cannon bombardment hit its target, Pickett's Charge would have, in all likelihood, been a successful strategy for General Lee. In fact, had the Charge been successful, the Confederacy may well have won the Battle of Gettysburg, possibly changing not only the outcome of that battle, but of the war and the future of our country.

Instead, his cannons aimed too high and the rest is history. Think of your credit cards as cannonballs. Aim too high by purchasing more than you can afford to pay off at the end of the month, and your creditors are free to mow you down just as the Union forces decimated Pickett's Brigade. Use your credit cannons wisely, aim at only what you can afford, and you will be well on the way to marching into a secure retirement.

CHAPTER 4
WEALTH KILLERS: TAXES AND INFLATION

"The taxpayer—that's someone who works for the federal government but doesn't have to take the civil service examination."

RONALD REAGAN

"It's not how much you make, it's how much you keep."

ANON

The Battle of Gettysburg claimed approximately 51,000 Union and Confederate casualties after only three days of bloody fighting. When the battle began, a civilian named Jennie Wade and her family fled their home to avoid being in the direct line of fire. They decided to take refuge at her sister's house on Baltimore Street on the outskirts of town. As the Union retreated to Cemetery Hill, the family found themselves once again in the midst of the battle. Despite the danger from sniper bullets striking the house walls, Jennie continued to provide water and bread to the Union troops manning the picket lines nearby. As Jennie stood in her sister's kitchen early on the morning of July 3rd baking a batch of bread, she was struck down by a Confederate sniper's bullet, becoming the lone civilian casualty of that infamous battle. Despite her efforts to avoid the dangers of war, she unfortunately fond that some situations in life are inescapable.

Unfortunately for you, there are "snipers" taking aim at your financial savings and investment income. One of your enemies is taxes, and the other is a notorious silent enemy called inflation. You can attempt to ignore the dangers of these two killers like Jennie Wade and in the end, like her, become trapped in the battle without a chance for escape. Or, you can scan the horizon; recognize the snipers and work to minimize the danger to your financial health.

TAXES: CONTROL THEM BEFORE THEY CONTROL YOU

Let's start with the wealth killer that everyone is aware of called taxes. We all pay some form of federal, state, and local taxes on our income annually. We can't ignore the taxman, but wise warriors look for ways to make the tax laws work for them so they can minimize fiscal casualties. Education is the premier weaponry to arm you against the relentless and never-ending tax battle. And believe it or not, this is something you can take control of, before it takes control of you.

In order to diminish the effectiveness of the taxman, you must have a number of powerful weapons such as an understanding of tax laws and their associated vocabulary in your financial arsenal. The savvy investment warrior knows that he should not fight this battle alone. Recruit a reputable financial advisor and certified public accountant into your army to team with you to ensure that tax laws work for you and not against you. Let's map out a battle strategy that will enable you to build a financial arsenal against the tax invasion.

ITEMIZE YOUR RETURN USING ALL ELIGIBLE DEDUCTIONS

Determine if it is advantageous for you to itemize your tax return rather than taking the standard deductions. To determine if itemization is the right strategy, take your gross income minus all allowable deductions. This figure will be your taxable income. Then calculate your taxable income using your gross income minus the standard deductions. Legitimate deductions for itemizing may include but are not limited to personal exemptions, state and local income taxes, property taxes, investment losses, casualty or theft losses, mortgage interest paid, charitable contributions, and business and moving expenses for which you were not reimbursed.

You may also benefit from itemizing tax credits and adjustments which may apply to your particular situation. Tax adjustments can be alimony payments, student loan interest, and eligible contributions to a traditional IRA. Additionally, tax credits may be available for child and dependent care expenses, costs associated with adoption foreign taxes paid, and educational expenses.

Now that you can see the value in itemizing to minimize your tax bill, you can start to build a strategy for saving tax dollars as early as this year. As always, my best advice is to team with your financial advisor and CPA, who can assist you in determining the effectiveness of this strategy.

EMPLOYER-SPONSORED RETIREMENT PLAN

If you are not already participating in your employer-sponsored retirement plan, you are missing out on an important defense against the taxman. The current most popular company-sponsored retirement plans are 401(k) for private business and the 403(b) plan for the public sector. In both cases, your contributions are deducted from your gross earnings pre-tax. Additionally, the principal and interest in a 401(k) or 403(b) retirement plan are tax deferred until you withdraw the funds. Presumably, you will have less income during retirement, and therefore, the taxes you will eventually pay on your retirement account will be taxed in a lower bracket. One last note: if you are self-employed, there are a multitude of vehicles the federal government has provided for you to save on a tax-deferred basis. As an example, you could potentially be able to deduct up to $45,000 in 2007 by using a 401(k) Profit Sharing plan.

UTILIZE EMPLOYER-SPONSORED PRETAX DEDUCTIONS

Some employers offer pre-tax deductions for health, dental, and vision insurance and accounts that allow you to make deductions for medical and childcare expenses for which you were not reimbursed. An example would be a Flexible Spending Account (FSA). The amount set aside must be determined in advance, and employees lose any unused dollars in the account at year-end.

Another outstanding benefit, which is relatively underused and unknown, is the Health Savings Account (HSA). The HSA allows you to set aside pre-tax dollars for future medical, retirement, or long-term care premium expenses. You can invest these funds into a broad range of choices such as mutual funds or money market accounts. The unused funds can roll over from year to year. To be eligible for an HSA, you must be enrolled in a qualified medical plan with a high deductible.

CONTRIBUTE TO A TRADITIONAL IRA

A traditional IRA is the most popular and an excellent way to defer taxes while saving for retirement. If your employer does not sponsor a 401(k) or 403(b) plan, work with your financial advisor to find the best IRA program to win the war against income decay. Your financial advisor or your CPA will apprise you of any income restrictions. If you meet these restrictions, you may deduct your IRA contributions from your tax liability. And your IRA money grows tax-deferred until withdrawn.

LOSSES CAN BE YOUR GAIN

Bad year in the market? You sold some of your securities for less money than you paid for them? The good news is that you now have a capital loss that is tax deductible, provided the securities were in a taxable account. In most cases you may deduct up to $3,000 of your losses to offset your tax liability in any given year. If your losses exceed $3,000, you may be able to carry the difference over to offset gains in future years. Such loss carryover has no expiration date.

TIMING: WHEN TO BUY/SELL MUTUAL FUNDS

Talk with your financial planner to determine when to buy and sell mutual funds. Timing can have major implications for capital gains tax. Let me illustrate.

I had a prospect come to me back in February 2001. She was complaining that she had just received her 1099 and

it showed that she had a huge amount of taxes to pay. The problem was that she actually lost money the previous year and couldn't understand why she had to pay taxes. After reviewing her accounts, which were at another brokerage firm, I noticed she had purchased mutual funds on November 15, 2000. This happened to be the record date of the mutual fund that she owned. That meant she had to pay a portion of the capital gains and dividend taxes the mutual fund had realized throughout the year. Even though she had not participated in these gains, she still had to pay her share. It just so happened that her tax bill that year was over $300,000, and unfortunately she never made a penny. OUCH!

INFLATION: THE SILENT ENEMY

Inflation is a different type of sniper known as the silent enemy. You can't hide from or totally diversify away from inflation. The best you can do is to recognize its presence by attempting to estimate the cost of goods and services in the coming years. The longer you live, the more inflation will erode your initial investments. This is the main reason why you will need more money to live comfortably in retirement. The battle strategy here is realizing that it is not how much you "earn" that is important, but how much you get to "keep" of that income you earned. We refer to this concept as the Real Rate of Return (ROR), and this awareness will help you keep pace with inflation. Suppose you had a 10% rate of return on your investment. If your federal tax bracket is 25% and you combine that with 3% inflation, after taxes and inflation, the ROR is approximately 4.4% (you also may be hit with state income taxes).

Many of us tend to "play it safe" with our investments.

Like a soldier in a bunker, we hunker down with Certificates of Deposits (CDs), minimal interest-bearing savings accounts, low-interest bonds, and/or stable funds inside a 401(k) or 403(b) account, thinking that we are safe from the sniper. But I'd like to say a CD is not an acronym for a Certificate of Deposit but more like a Certificate of Depreciation. Ironically, it can lock you into a rate of interest less than inflation, allowing you to go broke...and may I add...safely. Your money in the bank is working FOR the bank and not you. Inflation not only taxes your gain, but also your principal.

Let me illustrate how a CD is affected by taxes and inflation.

CD Value:	$10,000
Earning Rate:	x 8%
Interest Earned Annually:	$800
Inflation Rate:	5%
Federal Tax Rate:	28%
State Tax Rate:	+ 7%
Annual Tax/Inflation:	40%
Interest Earned Annually:	$800
Annual Tax/Inflation:	x 40%
After Tax Amount:	$480

I almost forgot you were also taxed by inflation on your principal. That means you lost another $500 (5% of 10,000) in spending power. So you made a net return of $480 on your interest, and you lost $500 on your principal. Guess what? Your net spending power is: $9,980. Now you know why I call them Certificates of Depreciation. And remember, that's at 8%. Find me an 8% interest-bearing CD today!

Another "voice" to learn from:

One client began his sales career at a major tire manufacturer. This company had a defined pension plan that vested at the end of ten years of employment. After seven years, this gentleman became disillusioned with his employer but felt he could not leave the company for another three years. His father had led him to believe that he must vest his pension before leaving. And so, for three long, miserable years, he stayed. And for what? At age 65, this "wonderful" pension is netting $100 a month!

It simply never occurred to this client that inflation would be eating away at his pension and that $100 in 1968 bought a whole lot more than it buys today. It is important to note that this pension did not offer a Cost Of Living Adjustment (COLA).

Generally, you can use four percent annually to estimate the injury inflicted by inflation to your "safe" investment accounts. When fighting the silent enemy, the best offense is NOT a defense. Establishing a diversified investment portfolio is the only way your money can grow. Otherwise you are simply letting inflation erode your money like rust eating through a strong material like lead. Eventually, you will find yourself without cannonballs to fight your battles. The value of your money today will continue to shrink into the future.

DIMINISHING FIRE POWER: The devaluation of $5,000 eroding at a 4% per-annum inflation rate

```
TODAY = $5,000
   10 YEARS = $3,378
      20 YEARS = $2,282
         30 YEARS = $1,514
```

Historically, inflation rises and falls each year based on a number of factors too complicated to mention. But one certainty is the unpredictability of how much inflation will rise. As an example, in 1986 inflation was at a rock bottom annual rate of 1.1%. All you had to do to beat inflation was to top 1.1% and hopefully more to ensure your money was not decaying. However, in the subsequent 4-year period that followed, inflation rose 4.4%, 4.4%, 4.6%, and 6.1% respectfully. A pattern of unpredictability for sure that required your money to work harder during that era to stay ahead of the deadly pace. The long-term picture reveals that inflation has moved upward at an average of 3% over the past 20 years from 1985 to 2005. All inflation data has been based on the Consumer Price Index.

Understanding inflation is half the battle when preparing for retirement. It's estimated that your retirement expenses could be as high as 80% of your current expenses today. We need to dispel a very dangerous myth right now, which has many believing that their expenses at retirement will fall considerably. The silent enemy of inflation has already exposed a decaying dollar in the future coupled with the price of (practically) everything rising. Even if you anticipate some expenses going away and nothing being added to negatively impact your budget, experts believe you'll still need to assume your expense line to be comparable to what it is today. Let me break down the scenario with a few assumptions.

Current Monthly Expenses: $6,000
Inflation Rate Over 15 Years: 4%
Life Expectancy after Retiring: 30 years

Step 1
$6,000 (current monthly expenses)
x .80 (80% projected expenses at retirement)
$4,800 (projected dollars needed monthly for
expenses at retirement)

Step 2
$4,800 (projected retirement expenses)
x1.801 (4% inflation factor over the 15 years leading
up to retiring)
$8,645 (inflation adjusted projected expenses at
retirement)

Step 3
$8,645(inflation adjusted projected expenses at
retirement)
x   12(months)
$103,740(annual projected retirement expenses)

So let's assume you get a 6% rate of return on your investments and inflation remains at 4% per year; how much of a lump sum will you need at retirement to produce the income in the above example? $500,000? $750,000? $1,000,000? Actually, you will need close to $2,000,000 saved up to be able to continue spending that amount of money. This illustration assumes you have already taken into account the amount of other income you will be getting in retirement (i.e. Social Security, pensions, etc.). The example also assumes that you will live for 30 years in retirement, die at age 90 with no money, and the interest and inflation compounds annually. Don't leave this to chance. You may be fine and saving the correct amount, but spend time and do the calculations and see if you are on track.

Diversify and invest your money wisely to keep those deadly financial snipers away. Remain in the line of battle without a strategy like Jennie Wade, and you will eventually succumb to the assassins against your wealth.

CHAPTER 5
INVENTORY FOR THE RETIREMENT BATTLE:
SOURCES OF INCOME

"The question isn't at what age I want to retire, it's at what income."

GEORGE FOREMAN

Physical and financial survival for the soldiers at Gettysburg came from three sources: army pay, packages from home, and foraging from the civilian population or opposition casualties. Army pay earned on a monthly basis was to be distributed bi-monthly; however, the receipt of payment was likely to be sporadic. Monthly Union pay rates ranged from $13.00 for a private to $758 for a three-star general. A Confederate private received $11.00 a month, but a rebel general's salary was comparable to the Union.

Packages from home were highly anticipated and greatly appreciated by the soldiers from both sides. A typical care package might include a new shirt, socks, soap, towels, and writing supplies.

Foraging was the main source of sustenance for an army on the move. Soldiers confiscated livestock, chickens, horses, and food from the civilian population in the battle zone. Both Confederate and Union soldiers "raided" casualties for their clothing, shoes, weapons, and supplies. Most prized among the Johnny Rebs were the Union "gum blankets," rubber-coated cloths that were used as sleeping pads.

While life for today's retiree is very different from that of the soldiers of Gettysburg, they do have a three-pronged income method in common. Visualize if you will a three-legged stool. One leg of the Gettysburg stool would be army pay. The second leg would represent care packages. The third leg needed to balance the three-legged stool of a soldier is foraging. In traditional times the legs of the stool would be made up of savings, social security and company pensions. Today, we find the legs of the stool to represent savings, social security, and 401(k)/403(b) plans. Let me explain in more detail. While the army supplied part of a soldier's monetary requirements and daily rations, they depended upon the voluntary generosity of family and the not-so-voluntary generosity of civilians and casualties. During succeeding generations, the onus switched to the government and the employer. More workers had access to company-sponsored, defined benefit retirement plans, and most, if not all, depended upon Social Security to provide a large percentage of their retirement incomes. Today, the pendulum is swinging back in the direction of self-reliance. Without delving into the political soup of the health of the current Social Security system, if you are depending heavily on the Social Security leg for a high percentage of retirement income in the later part of the century, you may find that leg shorter than the other two, or broken altogether. Try sitting on a two-legged or unbalanced stool! Additionally, more and more employers are eliminating or phasing out defined benefit retirement plans in favor of 401(k) or 403(b) plans that put the onus on the employee to participate and contribute. Saving for the purpose of retirement income includes traditional savings accounts, individual retirement accounts (IRAs), and investments.

Like the soldier at Gettysburg, make certain you know the most important things to have in your retirement income haversack.

INDIVIDUAL RETIREMENT ACCOUNTS (IRAS)

Even if you are lucky enough to still have an employee-sponsored, defined benefit retirement plan, you may want to establish an IRA account. You need to know that there are two types of IRAs: the **TRADITIONAL** and the **ROTH**.

The **Traditional IRA** can be used for retirement savings if:

- **Your employer does not have an employer-sponsored retirement plan.**

- **You are already making the maximum allowable contribution to your employer-sponsored plan.**

- **Your spouse has no earned income but wants to save for retirement.**

- **You change jobs and are required to remove or consolidate your accumulated retirement funds from the employer-sponsored plan.**

Additional eligibility rules include:

- **You must be under the age of 70.5 years and have earned income in the year you contribute to an IRA.**

- **You may contribute 100% of your earned income up to a maximum of $4,000 per year. There is no minimum contribution.**

- **Your non-working spouse can contribute up to**

$4,000 a year. There is no minimum contribution.

- You and your spouse can contribute a maximum of $8,000 a year even if you both are employed. There is no minimum contribution.

- If over age 50, you may contribute an additional $1,000 to catch up.

- You may make your contributions to an IRA as late as April 15th for the previous year.

As stated in the previous chapter, traditional IRAs offer great tax savings. Not only are the earnings tax deferred, but you may also be able to deduct the contribution. Look at the following table to see if you are able to make a tax deduction.

- A working spouse of a married couple contributing to an employer-sponsored fund cannot deduct. A non-working spouse who doesn't contribute may deduct; however, the total income of the couple must be under $160,000.

- IRA withdrawals not subject to penalty, prior to the age of 59.5 years, can be made for educational expenses, first-time home purchase up to $10,000, for qualified medical expenses, or for death or disability. Distributions that are in a series of equal payments may also qualify.

- IRA principal and interest grow tax deferred until the funds are withdrawn.

- After the age of 59.5 years, you may take penalty-free withdrawals from your IRA. Remember that taxes on the earnings and the contributions (if they were made tax-deferred) are due when you withdraw from the IRA account. If you deduct before the age of 59.5, there is an additional 10% penalty.

- If you don't begin the required minimum distribution (RMD) by April 1st after reaching 70.5 years of age, you will be penalized 50% of what your distribution should have been.

The second type of IRA, known as the **ROTH IRA**, was created by the Taxpayer Relief Act of 1997. You may want to consider establishing and contributing to a Roth IRA if:

- Your adjusted gross income is above the limit eligible for a tax deduction to a traditional IRA.

- Your employer does have a company-sponsored defined contribution retirement plan (i.e. 401(k), 403(b)).

- You want to continue working and making IRA contributions beyond age 70.5 years.

- You are now close to retirement but do not want to make withdrawals by age 70.5.

- May want to supplement your budget in retirement with tax-free income.

Like the traditional IRA, the Roth IRA has advantages, disadvantages, and participation rules and contribution limits.

- Roth contributions must be made using after-tax dollars but earning grows tax deferred.
- A non-working spouse can contribute up to $4,000 annually.

- Contributions came be made up to April 15th for the preceding year.

- Since you do not have to begin making withdrawals from a Roth IRA at age 70.5, you have more flexibility in planning your tax liability during retirement.

- Your contributions and earnings can be withdrawn tax free, if you meet a five-year holding period and age restrictions.

- If over age 50, you may do an additional $1,000 catch-up.

Income Limitations for ROTH IRA Contributions (2006)

	Married Filing Jointly	Single Filer	Married Filing Separately
Full Contribution	Income less than $150,000	Income less than $95,000	None
Contribution less than $4,000	Income $150,000 to $160,000	Income $95,000 to $110,000	Income $0 to $10,000
Contribution not allowed	Income above $160,000	Income above $110,000	Income above $10,000

A traditional IRA may be converted to a Roth IRA, but there are pros and cons. If you convert, you must pay the income tax at the time of conversion at your current rate.

When you convert a traditional IRA, funded with tax-deductible contributions to a Roth IRA, you will pay taxes on both the contributions and the earnings; however, if the traditional IRA was funded with non-deductible dollars, you will pay taxes only on the earnings. Think very carefully before you decide to convert. And if you do, you may want to convert your traditional IRA over the course of several years. It is likely that you will then pay less total tax than if you converted in a single year. In order to convert, your AGI must be under $100,000 if you are married filing jointly or a single filer.

SOCIAL SECURITY INCOME

Here's a little history lesson. Did you know that President Franklin Roosevelt signed the Social Security Act into law in 1935? Shortly thereafter, the American worker began using Social Security benefits to fund retirement. As demographics shifted and baby boomers now approach retirement, it has been necessary to make a multitude of changes to the system. As time goes on, the ratio of workers to Social Security beneficiaries is slowly eroding.

The Impending Bust of Social Security
1945   42 workers to 1 beneficiary
2004   3.3 workers to 1 beneficiary
2030   2.2 workers to 1 beneficiary

The Social Security system sends regular statements that detail your retirement benefits and age restrictions for drawing Social Security. Since you receive this information and keep it on file with your other important retirement information, it is not necessary, for our purposes, to repeat it here. You should, however, be certain to check and make sure the numbers on the report are accurate.

Below is a chart that indicates how much of your Social Security benefit you'd receive at age 62, depending of course on the year in which you were born. The last column indicates when you are entitled to full benefits.

Birth Year	% of Retirement Available at Age 62	Full Retirement Age (Year/Month)
1938	79.17	65/2
1939	78.33	65/4
1940	77.50	65/6
1941	76.67	65/8
1942	75.83	65/10
1943-1954	75.00	66/0
1955	74.16	66/2
1956	73.34	66/4
1957	72.50	66/6
1958	71.67	66/8
1959	70.83	66/10
1960 or Later	70.00	67/0

Some people elect to retire at age 62 and begin collecting a portion of their Social Security benefit before reaching 100% eligibility. For example, a person born between 1943 and 1954 can collect 75¢ on the dollar for four years before reaching the full retirement age of 66.

Also, you will not only receive a reduction in your benefit, you may also be penalized if you return to work. For example, for the year 2006 when you reach age 62 to the end of the year prior to full retirement age, you will lose $1 for every $2 dollars earned over $12,480. In the year you reach full retirement age, you will lose $3 for every $1 you earn over $33,240. However, you will lose nothing starting with the month you reach full retirement age regardless of the amount of money you earn. In 2007 the limit will increase to $12,960 and $34,440 respectively.

Here is an example of someone who retired at age 62, started receiving Social Security, and decided to go back to work earning $35,000 per year.

Returning To Work At	Age 62[3]	3)This assumes the person was born in 1944 and retired on his 62nd birthday. Social Security maximum monthly benefit in 2006 for a person retiring at age 62 is $1,540.
Earnings	$35,000	
Social Security Limit[4]	$12,480	
Excess Earnings	$22,520	
Gross Annual Social Security Benefit	$18,477	
Less Reduction	$11,260	4)2006 limits are used in this illustration. The amounts are adjusted annually.
Net Annual Social Security benefit	$7,217	

In 1993, the Revenue Reconciliation Act was enacted, which increased the taxable portion of Social Security benefits up to 85% depending on a person's income. Keep in mind that Social Security benefits are calculated differently than taxable income. Basically you take your adjusted gross income, plus non-taxable interest, plus one-half of your Social Security benefits. Please remember it is helpful to team with a CPA or tax specialist for assistance. Below is a chart showing the amount of Social Security that is taxable, depending upon the level of income.

BENEFITS THAT ARE TAXABLE	SINGLE FILER	MARRIED FILING JOINTLY
0%	Below $25,000	Below $32,000
Up to 50%	$25,000 - $34,000	$32,000 - $44,000
Up to 85%	Above $34,000	Above $44,000

EMPLOYER-SPONSORED RETIREMENT PLANS

There are retirement plans that qualify under IRS standards for favorable tax treatment. One type is called a **Defined Benefit Plan**, better known as a "Pension Plan," in which the employer controls most of the investment process. Some elements of this type of plan are:

- Defined monthly benefit to eligible retirees

- Formulas used are based on salary, years of service, etc. or exact dollar issuance

- Most are protected by the Pension Benefit Guaranty Corporation (PBGC)

- Employees may or may not be required to contribute to the plan

- Participants are not required to select investment options

- Retirement income is usually taxed as ordinary income upon withdrawal

- Annual distribution from the Plan must occur after age 70½

There are several advantages to a defined benefit plan, with one being the responsibility of the employer to provide the retirement benefit. The employee knows in advance what the amount of the benefit will be and is not required to contribute, which leaves no investment risk. Plan assets are managed by professional money managers and offer tax-deferred retirement savings. Some provide a cost of living adjustment, and if insured, PBCG guarantees a portion of the earned benefit if the employer cannot afford to pay.

On the other hand, there are several disadvantages to these types of plans. In particular, no individual accounts are established for the employees, which may provide only a portion of funds needed for retirement. Often these plans are difficult to understand, not to mention that they usually don't benefit employees who leave before retirement. Benefits are typically not payable until normal retirement age, and most plans do not permit lump sum payments at retirement.

The Defined Benefit Plan has become a dinosaur in organizations' benefit packages because they are costly to the employer who is guaranteeing payment. In turn, **Defined Contribution Plans** have become more prevalent because they make "you," the employee, responsible for retirement investment through 401(k) or 403(b) plan types, to name two. Although there are some very minor differences between the two, the main difference is that 401(k) plans are found in "for-profit" organizations and 403(b) plans in "non-profit" organizations.

In general, these plans allow employees to contribute pre-tax dollars to reduce their annual taxable income and are usually made through payroll deduction. Until withdrawn, the earnings grow tax deferred, and employees are able to select and change their investment funds during the years of contribution. Fees are usually built into the plans with professional fund managers handling the portfolios. Most plans allow employees to choose from a list of professionally managed mutual funds. Beneficiary selection can be changed, and some employers will match employee contributions. If your employer provides a match, make sure you are contributing enough to receive the entire match. If you don't, you are throwing away free money. Each year, the employee must be aware of the contribution limit allowed by the IRS. In 2007, for example, the employee contribution limit was $15,500 with a $5,000 catch-up clause allowed for employees over the age of 50. The combined total of profit sharing and retirement contributions cannot exceed 100% of the employee's annual compensation or $45,000 (2007 figure). Again, the annual dollar limit can vary from year to year.

An employee's investment contribution and earnings are 100% vested (how much you are allowed to keep), while the employer's share may occur over a graded process or time schedule.

Withdrawals can be made for "qualifying" reasons such as death, disability, or financial hardship prior to the age of 59½ without a 10% penalty. Your tax advisor should be consulted if you are contemplating withdrawing any funds before age 59½. However, withdrawals may occur penalty free if you leave your employer in the year you turn 55 or after, under the auspices of retirement. If you do plan to retire before age 55 and wish to take payments, they must be Substantially Equal Periodic Payments (SEPP) and continue for more than five years or until you reach age 59½ to avoid a penalty. Withdrawals made between the ages of 59½ and 70 are subject to tax as ordinary income. After you reach age 70½ and you are no longer working, you must begin to take minimum distributions from your 401(k) or 403(b) plan. Finally, the employee may have the ability to take loans against his or her account with restrictions. In any scenario, it is the employee's responsibility to be educated on the annual dollar figures and penalties set by the IRS.

While I have mentioned only two types of Defined Contribution Plans, there are others such as SEPs, SIMPLEs, and 457 plans.

OTHER SOURCES OF RETIREMENT INCOME

Many of us will have other sources of retirement income depending on what we bought, invested in, or saved during our working years. Some examples of additional income include:

Employment Income – Many retirees elect to work full- or part-time, depending upon their health and other activities. If you plan to continue working, be aware of any maximum earnings limitations on your pension and/or Social Security. Remember that employment income can reduce Social Security and/or pension benefits and possibly create a tax liability.

- **Home Equity – This is the value of your house minus what you owe on the mortgage. There are opportunities to turn this equity into retirement income, particularly in the case of a reverse mortgage. A reverse mortgage might be very beneficial to you, but you will absolutely want to check with your financial experts before deciding to enter into a reverse mortgage.**

- **Rental Property – Maybe you own a vacation home that you rent out, or maybe you have invested in rental property during your working years. Regardless, there is potential for added retirement income from these properties, which may present you with opportunities for capital gains and depreciation as well as income. It is important to know the ins and outs for your tax planning during retirement.**

- **Inheritances – Haven't we all dreamed about a long-lost, rich relative leaving us a bundle of money to put our retirement on Easy Street? It's possible that you have or will inherit funds that can be invested and** add to your retirement income. If I were you, this is the one form of additional personal income I'd count on the least.

- Investments – Simply defined as monies outside of your retirement plan or IRAs that can be an important vehicle for funding retirement. Investments might include annuities, bonds, certificates of deposit, and/or mutual funds. Investments should not be stagnant, and therefore you shouldn't leave them unattended. As circumstances in your financial life change, you need to look at your current investments and adjust your strategy. Later we'll talk about investments in more detail.

Hopefully by now, you have already begun to think about what you want to have in your financial arsenal and have taken the appropriate steps to become as financially self-reliant as those brave soldiers at Gettysburg. And just in case I haven't made my point yet, General Robert E. Lee from the Confederate Army and Major General George G. Meade from the Union Army didn't devise their battle strategies in isolation. They relied on the best information they could gather through cavalry reconnaissance, battlefield observation, and discussions with their trusted subordinates. Going into the retirement battle without trusted financial advisors is like a soldier marching down the Chambersburg Pike without ammunition or a haversack. Talk to your trusted advisors and pack what they recommend, and you will live well to tell the tale. Remember, it is more important to be a good saver than it is to be a good investor.

CHAPTER 6
EMPTYING THE RETIREMENT HAVERSACK:
RETIREMENT FUND DISTRIBUTIONS

"I have enough money to last me the rest of my life, unless I buy something."

JACKIE MASON

Governments of both the North and South spent great sums of money to provide rations for their troops. In *Echoes from the Marches of the Famous Iron Brigade*, author Cullen Bryant Aubrery listed rations purchased during 1863, the year of the Battle of Gettysburg. Among an extensive list were items such as these for the Seventh Wisconsin regiment Old Iron Brigade:

1,337 barrels of pork - 29,694 pounds of bacon - 35,593 pounds of ham - 528 pounds of fresh beef - 742 cattle slaughtered - 1,748 barrels of flour - 487,307 pounds of hard bread - 1,764 pounds of cornmeal - 60,820 pounds of beans - 9,336 pounds of rice - 16,420 pounds of dried apples - 884 pounds of dried peaches - 55,565 pounds of coffee - 715 pounds of tea - 124,898 pounds of brown sugar - 917 pounds of white sugar - 8,659 pounds of candles - 18,007 pounds of soap - 19,672 pounds of salt - 571 pounds of pepper - 24,241 gallons of vinegar - 1,062 gallons of pickles - 232 cabbages - 458 gallons whiskey - 2,080 dried vegetables – 20,436 pounds of potatoes - 7,962 onions - 3,210 beets - 2,782 turnips - 1,158 pounds of carrots.

"The average number of men was 1,863, a daily cost per man of 24½¢. This included the feeding of the One Hundred and Sixty-seventh Pennsylvania Militia, who were attached from July 17th to Aug. 5th. (51-52)."

You probably won't be feeding an army, but like the Seventh Wisconsin, you will need to procure goods and services after your retirement. Perhaps you will need money for mortgage payments and social activities. Certainly you will need to buy food and clothing, and health services. As discussed in Chapter 5, you have prepared for these expenditures by putting money in your "retirement haversack" through a pension plan, an IRA, a 401(k) or a 403(b) account. There are several criteria that govern the removal of your funds from your "haversack," and it is important to understand these criteria and any governmental or fund limitations in order to maximize your resources and tax position, as well as avoid losing principal through penalties.

RETIRING OR CHANGING JOBS

First let's look at withdrawing funds from either a defined benefit plan or a defined contribution plan if you are retiring from one position and taking another one that will have a retirement plan.

DEFINED BENEFIT PLAN

A defined benefit plan promises a monthly benefit beginning at normal retirement age. There may be a formula for calculating this monthly annuity tied to salary history and years of service, or the plan may state a definitive monthly allotment. If you are vested in a defined benefit plan and have not yet reached the normal retirement age as specified in your plan, you may leave your money there until you are ready to receive monthly payments at retirement age. Check with your company's benefit specialist <u>before</u> making a withdrawal option decision.

While your plan may specify a number of different options, at the least you will need to specify your choice between single life or joint and survivor options. The single life option will increase your monthly income, but will cease payment upon your death. Think back to the elderly lady from the Gettysburg Diner, whom I introduced to you in the foreword of this book. Her husband elected the single life coverage and left his aged widow with no income other than Social Security. Recalling her story may indicate that a survivor option is always the preferred choice for a married couple. Not so! Your selection needs to be based on a sound analysis of your total financial picture, including tax liability. A word of caution: once you make a selection, generally you can not change it. Make certain that both you and your spouse are comfortable with your choice. Let me illustrate this important concept with two "voices."

> **One couple, both in their late sixties, owns a mortgage-free home valued at $750,000. The pensioner, in this case the husband, also has a life insurance policy worth $100,000; his wife is the beneficiary. In addition, the couple owns several rental properties, which provide a monthly income of $600 each. The wife worked for many years for a government agency and has both a Social Security and a pension in her own name. If the husband elected the single life option, his monthly annuity would**

be $3,240. If he chose the joint and survivor option, the monthly annuity would decrease to $2,375 — a difference of $865. After carefully analyzing their total financial situation, this couple agreed that the wife would have ample income to support her needs if her husband should predecease her, and determined it would better suit them to select the single life option and use the addition $865 per month to travel, one of their main retirement objectives.

The second couple is also in their late sixties; however, they had to purchase a larger home five years ago to accommodate her elderly mother living with them. They will still have a considerable mortgage at retirement. The wife has never worked outside of the home and, therefore, has no retirement funding of her own. She can collect her husband's Social Security if he should die before her. Using the same retirement annuity figures of either $3,240 or $2,375, this couple decided to use a large portion of the monthly difference of $865 to purchase life insurance.

The second couple chose a common financial planning tool known as pension maximization. You may find that you can purchase a substantial sum of life insurance that will leave the spouse in a better financial situation than if she had only the pension annuity. If you choose a survivor option or purchase a separate life insurance policy, you are insuring the on-going financial resources of your survivor. Please be certain that you qualify for the purchase of life insurance and have the policy fully implemented prior to selecting this option.

Some plans may also offer a third option called joint & 50% survivor. If we use the same monthly annuity figures, the three plans can be illustrated by the chart below:

Annuity Choice	Monthly Benefit	Monthly Survivor Benefit
Single Life	$3,240	$0
Joint & 100% Survivor	$2,375	$2,375
Joint & 50% Survivor	$2,000	$1,000

Some defined benefit plans offer two other options: *period certain* and *life with period certain*. A period certain annuity is distributed as a defined monthly payment for a specific number of years. When the time period ends, benefits cease. There are no survivor benefits with the election of this option.

A life with period certain option enables the retiree to collect the pension for his/her lifetime. Should the recipient die prior to the conclusion of the period specified in the plan, the spouse would receive monthly benefits until the end of the period.

Like the two "voice" families, make a prudent decision based upon your own needs and situations. The only right answer to whether you should chose the single life or one of the joint and survivor options is what is best for you and your spouse.

Another option some plans allow is the ability to take a lump sum distribution of your entire defined benefit plan. Most people who decide to take this option would transfer the money into a traditional IRA to avoid paying taxes. Before doing this I would strongly recommend you contact a competent financial professional, such as a Certified Financial Planner™. Once you take a lump sum, your income will no longer be guaranteed by your employer. You are on your own to invest the money wisely. While the disadvantage of taking a lump sum should be considered, there are some advantages. One, you will now be in control of how much income you can take. Two, if you don't need the income, you can invest it in your IRA and allow it to grow tax-deferred. Three, if you and your beneficiary do not use all the money, it can be passed on to another beneficiary. Most annuity payments will cease after the annuitant and their survivor die.

Let me illustrate the third advantage with a story:

A client of mine retired from a large corporation. He decided that he would continue to work at another company. Since he did not need his pension, he decided to take a lump sum and invest it in his traditional IRA. Unfortunately, he passed away, and his wife inherited the IRA. Since she is still working and has her own pension, there is a good chance she will never need the money. Had he taken the monthly annuity, once she passed away the payments would have stopped. Since he took the lump sum, and assuming she does not spend all the money, her kids will be able to inherit the money.

DEFINED CONTRIBUTION PLAN

As we discussed in Chapter Five, there are several types of defined contribution plans like the 401(k) and the 403(b). Retirement benefits are based upon the amount of money accumulated in your fund, plus or minus investment gains or losses. If you have a defined contribution plan and are changing jobs, you have several options:

Option #1 - Leave your money in the employer-sponsored defined contribution plan if you are allowed to do so. However, you cannot make any additional contributions to the account. You will continue to have the limited investment options specified in the plan, but you will maintain the tax-deferred status of the account and avoid any penalties for withdrawal. One potential drawback is that the defined contribution plan may change if your former employer is involved in a merger or a purchase or if the employer switches investment companies.

Option #2 - Transfer your accumulated money to your new employer's defined contribution plan. This will enable you to continue making tax-deferred contributions, but your investment options will be limited to those selected for the plan.

Option #3 - Take a lump sum payment. You pay taxes on the full amount of the account, but then invest your money any way you want.

Option #4 - Transfer your funds to a traditional IRA. You can continue making tax-deferred contributions, and you will have a broader range of investment options. Your investments may provide a hedge against inflation. You can access your money in case of an emergency, and your heirs have access to your account balance upon your death. This is a very important point! If you transfer your money to an IRA, make certain that the check is made payable to the IRA issuer, not you. Be forewarned, if you have the check made payable to you, you immediately incur the tax liability for the entire amount of the fund.

CONSIDERING EARLY RETIREMENT

As mentioned previously, if you are considering an early retirement, you need to be aware of the tax and penalty implications of withdrawing from your "haversack" before age 59.5 years. As a general rule, withdrawals from a traditional IRA made prior to 59.5 will incur a 10% tax penalty based on the amount you withdraw; taxes are payable when the money is taken.

We have already discussed several exceptions to this

rule: death, approved disability as defined by the IRS, money to cover medical expenses for which you were not reimbursed, totaling more than 7.5% of your adjusted gross income, and/or court-ordered distributions to an ex-spouse, child or dependent.

There are, however, a couple more common exceptions:

- **Distribution from a qualified plan, but not an IRA, upon termination of employment and retirement at the age of 55**

- **Internal Revenue Code Section 72(t) states that you may take approximately equal payments prior to age 59.5 years if you use one of three approved formulas: annuitization, amortization, or life expectancy to determine the amount of the equal payments. Once you have made a formula selection, you must remain with that formula for a minimum of five years or until you are 59.5, or whatever is longer. If not, you will have to pay a penalty tax plus interest on your IRA distributions**

Here is food for thought. If you retire at age 55 or older, but under age 59½, and need immediate access to your retirement funds, you can take a partial payment from your qualified plan, penalty free, at retirement and transfer the remainder of your fund balance in your IRA account.

WHEN MUST I BEGIN WITHDRAWALS FROM MY RETIREMENT FUNDS?

You must begin taking monetary distributions from your traditional IRA by April 1st of the year after you turn

70.5 years. The only exception is if you are still working for an employer with a sponsored plan; then you must begin making withdrawals by April 1st of the year after you retire.

The following table illustrates the minimum required distribution by age:

Age	Distribution Period	Age	Distribution Period
70	27.4 years	84	15.5 years
71	26.5 years	85	14.8 years
72	25.6 years	86	14.1 years
73	24.7 years	87	13.4 years
74	23.8 years	88	12.7 years
75	22.9 years	89	12.0 years
76	22.0 years	90	11.4 years
77	21.2 years	91	10.8 years
78	20.3 years	92	10.2 years
79	19.5 years	93	9.6 years
80	18.7 years	94	9.1 years
81	17.9 years	95	8.6 years
82	17.1 years	96	8.1 years
83	16.3 years	97	7.6 years

Here is another illustration from a voice of experience on the retirement battlefield:

An elderly gentlemen, age 84, had never taken a minimum distribution from his IRA. When the calculation of penalties and taxes were finished, he owed over $100,000! A very costly mistake, indeed.

You have grown your retirement funds through a government-approved, tax-deferred plan, but eventually the IRS is going to want their taxes. To minimize your tax liability, take only the minimum required distributions. If you do not take minimum distributions by age 70.5, you will incur a tax penalty of 50% of the difference between the minimum distribution and the money you actually withdrew. This can be a costly mistake!

The troops at the Battle of Gettysburg required a great deal of supplies to get them through the fight. Without the necessary resources they would have starved and not been able to wage war. Make sure you have stockpiled enough financial supplies so that you can be victorious on the Battlefield of Retirement.

CHAPTER 7
BUILDING A STRONG ARMY: INVESTMENTS

"Don't invest your money on the advice of a poor man."
SPAIN

I n his book, *Sleepless in New York*, author Tom Kalinke writes,

"Finding it difficult to borrow enough gold to finance the war, the federal government began, in early 1862, to pay some of its bills with currency ("greenbacks"). When the Union lost a battle, the price of gold in greenbacks went up. If the Union won a battle, the price went down. Telegraph lines from battle fronts to New York made the market's response time short; speculators were said to know battle results before President Lincoln.

"The price of gold swung wildly in the summer of 1862. The New York Stock Exchange (not the official name until January 29, 1863) acted "patriotically" by first banning time sales (settlements deferred up to 60 days), and then banning cash sales. The total ban lasted less than a month, but the combined moves were enough to end the see-saw volatility. Soon after gold trading resumed at the NYSE, the federal government began taxing gold sales with settlements longer than three days to discourage speculation.

"Speculation during the Civil War was not limited to gold. A bull market in stocks began in 1862 that extended into 1864, but the auction style of trading employed at the

61

NYSE was incapable of handling the increased trading volume. In addition, it was run like an exclusive club, meaning that a large number of brokers and traders could never hope to become members due to heritage or lack of influential friends. Some of these brokers tried forming their own exchanges."

One of the best known and most scandalous speculators of the time was Jim Fisk, a contemporary of John D. Rockefeller, Henry Flagler, Commodore C. Vanderbilt, and others who were great legends of American financial history. For many, such as Fisk, speculation was a costly adventure. Fisk discovered his partner, who was responsible for investing their gold profits, had put all of the money into Confederate bonds!

In 1932, Daniel Skelly published *A Boy's Experiences During the Battle of Gettysburg*, his outstanding eyewitness account of the Battle of Gettysburg from his perspective as a teenager. This excerpt explains how Daniel and his friend created their own version of profiteering, not all that different from Jim Fisk and his forage into gold speculation during the same period, but less risky and more profitable.

"On this morning, the 5th, my friend 'Gus' Bentley met me on the street and told me that down at the Hollinger warehouse where he was employed they had a lot of tobacco. 'We hid it away before the Rebs came into town,' he continued, 'and they did not find it. We can buy it and take it out and sell it to the soldiers.' Like all boys of those days we had little spending money but we concluded we would try and raise the cash in some way. I went to my mother and consulted her about it and she loaned me ten dollars. Gus also got ten, all of which we invested in the tobacco. It was in large plugs - Congress tobacco, a well-known brand at that time. With an old-fashioned tobacco cutter we cut it up into ten cent pieces and each of us took

a basket full and started out Baltimore Street to the cemetery, the nearest line of battle."

Although the law of supply and demand hasn't changed, the process of buying and selling stocks, bonds, and commodities has. You won't walk away from Chapter Seven as a successful day trader, nor will you know all the ins and outs of trading options. Others have produced excellent books on those topics if you want to learn more. But you should learn enough to keep from emulating Fisk's disaster and make a profit like Skelly. My goal is to give you a sound background in the basic foundation of investing: stocks and bonds.

DO YOU WANT TO BE FISK OR SKELLY?

First you must determine your reason or goal for investing. Are you looking for a large return or a steady income? Many "investors" ask friends or relatives for advice and then purchase based on that input. Others may select a fund for their 401(k)s by looking at what funds did best last year. Jim Fisk and his colleagues were looking to make a "killing" on their gold speculation, while Skelly and his friend were content to make a little spending money, a more modest profit. You will find it easier to select the right investments if you have a clear goal.

Simply put, the average person invests either stocks or bonds or has a financial portfolio that contains a combination of the two types of investments. What they usually don't know is why. When we talk about investing in stocks and bonds, there are two categories of investments: ownership or loanership.

LOANERSHIP INVESTMENT: BONDS

When you make a "loanership" investment, you purchase a bond. You expect the issuer to return your original purchase price plus interest, the premium the issuer pays you for letting him use your money for a while. Before you purchase a bond, you need to understand the following terms:

Face Value – This is the amount of money you pay for the bond. You may sometimes hear face value referred to as par value.

Coupon Rate – Amount of interest to be paid on a specific bond.

Yield – The annual percentage rate for your investment.

Maturity Date – The date on which the issuer agreed to repay your principal.

The Term – The time period between when the bond is issued and its maturity date.

Par – The value of a bond at original issue and will return in principal if held to maturity.

Premium Discount – A selling price above par.

Discount – A selling price below par.

Let me illustrate how important it is to have at least a passing understanding of these terms before you invest in any of the many types of bonds, including corporate bonds, treasury notes, municipal bonds, savings bonds, tax-free bonds, etc. with one of our "voices" from the battlefield.

A very conservative investor bought only high-quality, corporate bonds, believing that there was minimal risk for her return on investment. Due to an emergency, she

needed her assets and cashed in the bonds. She was dismayed to discover that her cash-out yielded 8% less than the amount of money she originally used to purchase the bonds. Ms. Conservative immediately called me for an explanation. The simple answer is that she did not hold the bonds until their maturity date in 22 years. So her investment actually turned into a loss. At the time, the market had dropped below her original purchase price.

Bonds and interest rates have an interesting relationship. Usually as the interest rate rises, the value of the bond falls and vice versa. In the above voice, interest rates were rising, lowering the value of her bond.

The two things that normally determine a bond's interest rate are the length of the term (maturity) and the buyer's credit rating. Let's talk a little about the credit rating. If you have excellent credit, you can secure a low-interest loan. Your neighbor may have a less-than-stellar credit history and must pay a higher rate of interest if he applies for a loan. Therefore, it holds true that if Company A has a bleak financial footing and wants to issue a bond, the issuer will have to pay higher interest. Since Company B is well situated financially, you will receive less interest on a bond issued by them. The direct link is the higher the risk, the higher the interest. When it comes to default risk, the least risky of all bond purchases are US government and municipal bonds.

Not being a financial wizard, how will you know if a company is in good standing? Several companies rate bonds; the two most popular are Standard & Poor's and Moody's. You can check their Web sites for current, accurate bond ratings.

Bonds with a low rating, normally BB/Ba or less, are commonly referred to as high-yield or "junk" bonds. The name "junk" became very popular during the '80s when Michael Milken transformed corporate takeover and financing by the use of high-yield bonds. Later a federal grand jury indicted Milken for violations of federal securities and racketeering laws. Now, don't let that scare you too much. It may be prudent to have some "junk" bonds in your investment portfolio, but only if managed by a reputable, professional fund manager due to the higher risk than the other types of bonds.

If you are risk-averse, high-grade corporate bonds, municipal bonds, and debt issued by the US Federal Government are probably your best choices. Remember, even though these types of bonds are very safe when it comes to the risk of default, inflation can eat away at their value at a fast rate.

In summary, investing in bonds provides stability and is historically less volatile than stocks. It also repays the principal and interest at maturity. The disadvantage to bond investing is that the rate of return is low compared to other investment options over the long haul. Also, there is no guarantee of return if the company fails.

LOANERSHIP INVESTMENT: CASH ACCOUNTS

There is a second option in the loanership category known as cash accounts. Cash accounts are commonly known by terms such as savings accounts, certificates of deposit, money market accounts, or money market mutual funds. These are viable investment options for anyone who needs to have ready access to cash in case of emergency.

Here are some characteristics of each of these accounts:

Savings Accounts, for example, provide unrestricted access to cash with a low minimum balance, insured up to $100,000 by FDIC. The downside is that these accounts pay low interest.

Certificates of Deposit restrict access to your money; and you may incur penalty on withdrawal; CDs pay a fixed interest rate; the longer the deposit is held, the higher the rate of return.

Money Market Accounts require a minimum balance; they offer variable interest rates and limited check writing privileges; they are usually insured by FDIC.

Money Market Mutual Funds are investments in government and corporate short debt. They are not insured by FDIC, they require a minimum balance and offer variable income. They do, however, offer check writing privileges.

A note about FDIC insurance: The $100,000 coverage limit pertains to a composite of all accounts you have in a particular bank, not to each individual account you may have. The exceptions may be joint accounts and retirement accounts such as IRAs.

Just like Fisk, he invested his money into high-yield confederate bonds. Remember, one of the disadvantages with bonds is the risk that the issuer of that bond won't pay back the principal (original investment). And in Fisk's case, the Confederacy failed and thus his bonds had no value due to the inability of "that" government to pay.

OWNERSHIP INVESTMENT

An ownership investment is actually the purchase of a portion of the stock-issuing company or what we commonly refer to as a stock share. This is different from a loanership investment where the individual lends money to a company or governmental agency through the purchase of a bond, which will return the principal at maturity. If your investment goals are growth, income, and tax benefits (capital gains), then ownership is a good option for you.

If you are a novice ownership investor, you might wonder why we even have a stock market. We'll let the "voice" of my father explain.

In 1982, my dad started his own company, Kissinger Financial Services. By 2001, he had built it into a very successful firm. But as a sole proprietor and like many small business owners, there were only a few ways he could get money for his investment. He could sell the business to a private buyer, or he could merge with a larger corporation. He also could become a publicly traded stock company or merge with a publicly traded stock company. That way, if he wanted or needed to remove some of his investment money, he could simply sell one or more shares of the company. That actually was the route he chose, and in April 2001, Kissinger Financial Services (KFS) merged with SMH Capital Inc. (SMHG). He received a number of stock shares in SMH equal to the value of KFS. This move allowed him full liquidity.

You might think of investing in bonds as emulating Daniel Skelly. Daniel and his friend invested a set amount of money (ten dollars each) with the hope for a return on this investment when they sold the tobacco. They understood that the risk was minimal because there were thousands of soldiers in and around Gettysburg who would gladly purchase their ten-cent plugs.

What the stock market does is bring willing buyers and willing sellers together just like the sutlers who followed the Union and Confederate armies. These traveling businesses stocked many of the necessities of the soldier's everyday life, such as soap, tobacco, razors, blankets, and gum sheets. The soldiers wanted to buy, the sutler wanted to sell; the "wagon shop" brought the two together. In the modern era, you might compare the stock market to eBay. Or you can think of it as a big yard sale held every day at the same location. In fact, there are three main markets in this country: the New York Securities Exchange (NYSE), the American Stock Exchange (ASE), and the National Association of Securities Dealers Automated Quotation System (NASDAQ). So it is really three big ongoing yard sales at different lawns.

We've all heard the "voices" of people who made small fortunes in the stock markets; they echo the "voices" of those who have lost money. For instance, many people made money in the 1920s, only to lose it in the Great Depression of the '30s. What makes the stock market rise and fall? Why is it so volatile? Stock market fluctuations are caused by many factors, such as a company reporting lower than anticipated profits, losing a big contract, revenue forecasting, or release of a new product. Inevitably, the price of a stock is determined by the laws of supply and demand. Naturally, if there are more buy orders, the price of the stock will go up. If few people want the stock, the selling prices per share will be lower.

You should have a basic knowledge of a few important stock terms.

Bears and Bulls – This term refers to recurring cycles of the stock market. A bear market describes a correction or downward trend in the market, while bull market describes an optimistic or upward trend. Need an easy way to remember the difference?

A bear stand on its hind legs and attacks downward at its victim. Thus a bear market is a pessimistic or downturn market.

A bull starts his charge with his head down and attacks his victim in an upward motion. So a bull market is one that is optimistic or upturning.

Daily action on the stock market is gauged by an index. The three most common indexes in our country are the Dow Jones Industrial Average, the Standard & Poor's 500 and the NASDAQ Composite Index. You can follow these indexes via television news or most daily newspapers and on the Internet. The average stock investor really doesn't need to know more than these few simple facts. But there are many resources, including books and classes, if you are interested in learning more.

When you identify your investment goals, you can choose to take great risks like Jim Fisk, or you can invest so that the risk of gain is managed like Daniel Skelly. I would greatly encourage you to work with a financial planner to help with the day-to-day management of your investment portfolio. Knowing your investment goals will aid you in making investment decisions that are right for you.

INVESTMENT VEHICLES FOR STOCKS & BONDS

There are countless types of investment choices to help you reach your monetary retirement objectives. You may elect to invest independently or buy into a mutual fund. I equate this to attempting to travel from point A to point B. You can elect to assume total accountability and control, and drive yourself. In investing, that means you do all the research and make the individual decisions to buy and sell. However, if you fall asleep at the wheel, you'll crash the car and never reach your goal. If you fall asleep at the wheel while investing, it will be detrimental to your retirement planning journey. On the other hand, if you take the bus, you'll still be going from point A to point B, but you are now commingling yourself with everyone else and therefore lessening the risk. The third example is the limousine theory. Let me explain these three types of investment vehicles from the standpoint of mutual funds, annuities, and separately managed accounts.

MUTUAL FUNDS

Currently there are thousands of mutual funds to choose from, and finding the right one takes doing some homework. However, the seemingly endless trail of mutual funds means that one or more are most likely tailored to your financial objectives. The diversification within a mutual fund coupled with professional portfolio management makes this road of financial travel less risky for the investor. The fund managers do all the research to buy and sell individual stocks/bonds to meet the overall objective of the fund itself. Some mutual funds can have upwards of several hundred different investments under one umbrella. Therefore, when you buy into a mutual fund, you may be buying a piece of many companies and corporations. More importantly, your money is pooled with many other investors like yourself, allowing the fund managers to buy and sell with greater financial leverage. These funds can also be structured to pay profits back to you by check, direct deposit, or automatic reinvestment. All the paperwork is done by the fund managers, and you receive periodic updates of your progress through notification and quarterly reports. As with most investments, any earnings get reported to the IRS even if they are being reinserted back into the fund. And one thing to remember, of course, is that the fund is only as good as the person responsible for its management. So be sure to research the track record of your portfolio manager to ensure s/he is the best person to be driving the bus for you. Finally, make sure you review the prospectus before investing.

ANNUITIES

There are two basic types of annuities: immediate and deferred. Both are contracts between you and the insurance company.

Immediate annuities are for retirees who make lump sum payments and in turn receive regular payments throughout the life of the contract. Pay schedules can be based on the investor's lifetime, a spouse's lifetime, or for a determined number of years.

Deferred annuities accumulate tax deferred until you begin to make withdrawals. A payment schedule is set to disperse income from the annuity back to you. As with most tax-deferred investment vehicles, certain restrictions apply, such as withdrawals before age 59½ that incur surrender charges and/or penalties. Also, guarantees to the investor are based on the ability of the insurance company to pay out claims.

A deferred annuity is categorized as fixed or variable. With the fixed annuity there are certain guarantees, such as principal, the minimum interest rate, and set (or fixed) income payments upon retirement, which equate to a safer investment mode. These annuities are often labeled tax-deferred CDs. Again, the guarantee of return is based on the insurance company's ability to pay out claims.

You may want to take more of a risk with greater potential through a variable annuity. The same withdrawal rules apply, with the main difference being the volatility of the investments to gain or lose more money similar to a mutual fund. You can select from among a list of professionally managed investment options, which are commonly called sub-accounts. Many people use variable annuities for the tax deferral and death-benefit protection. Most annuities guarantee at the death of the owner and/or annuitant the beneficiaries will receive the total premium payments minus withdrawals or the current market value, whichever is higher (check with each insurance company since policies and contracts differ). New advancements in variable annuities have tried to solve the risk of outliving your money by guaranteeing income for life and in some cases your spouse's.

Carefully review all material associated with an annuity contract before investing. **Annuities often have surrender charges and are normally priced higher than mutual funds.** Again, remember all the guarantees are based on the claim-paying ability of the issuing life insurance company.

INDIVIDUALLY MANAGED ACCOUNTS

Here the limo theory applies, where you invest in an individually managed account. These accounts usually carry a $100,000 minimum with the investor dictating the terms in regards to time, risk, and objectives for the manager to customize a portfolio. In this case there are no money pools, so the investor is a direct owner of each stock or bond in the portfolio. Tax-exempt investments may still be used to defer capital gains.

"Diamond Jim" Fisk lived and rode the financial roller coaster, going up and down, making and losing a vast fortune in risky investments. In contrast, Daniel Skelly became a successful Gettysburg businessman, making money the slow and safe way. Which one is right for you? I would suggest a combination of all three for a balanced portfolio, but it depends upon your personal situation. You should be an informed investor so that you can make the correct decision regarding what type of investment strategy will work best for you. The larger the portfolio, the more flexibility you will have, but there are so many vehicles to help you in your investing. Get educated, find a competent financial professional, and invest in the product that makes the most sense for your situation.

CHAPTER 8
IN THE EVENT OF AN AMBUSH: MANAGING THE RISK

"If you would be wealthy, think of saving as well as getting."
BENJAMIN FRANKLIN

The voice of military history echoes the depths of disaster when generals fail to manage risks. Consider the fateful Pickett's Charge as recounted by an anonymous military source.

"On July 3, Lee decided to press the attack to the Union center on Cemetery Ridge. At one in the afternoon, the southern artillery opened a bombardment that for a time engaged the massed guns of both sides in a thundering duel for supremacy, but did little to soften up the Union battle lines. Then came the climax of the Battle of Gettysburg...with a salute from Longstreet, General George E. Pickett, in a desperate attempt to recapture the partial success of the preceding day, spearheaded one of the most incredible efforts in military history...a massed infantry assault of 15,000 Confederate troops across the open field toward the Union center on Cemetery Ridge. One mile they marched, while being pounded by artillery and rifle fire. Through it all, Pickett's men reached but failed to break the Union line, and the magnificent effort ended in disaster. The tide of the Confederacy had 'swept to its crest, paused, and receded.' In 50 minutes, 10,000 in the assault had become casualties, and the attack — forever to be known as

Pickett's Charge — was now history."

Although General Lee and his command staff had done a superb job of managing their risks on the first two days of battle, he made three serious miscalculations on Day #3. He had underestimated the strength of the union forces, he had overestimated the number of available Confederate troops, and he expected his artillery to successfully clear the Union guns from their heights. Following the charge, General Lee inquired of Pickett about the location of his division. General Pickett replied, "Sir, I have no division."

You, too, must develop a plan for managing risk. There are two types of risk that we will be discussing: investment risks and life risks.

INVESTMENT RISKS

The first step in your strategic battle plan to cope with investment risk is to understand that you cannot eliminate all of the risk no matter what you do. Here's a "voice from the retirement battlefield" to share her story to illustrate this truth.

A very conservative woman decided to put all of her retirement savings in cash in a safety deposit box at her local bank. She had been a child of the depression and did not trust the stock market. Ms. Conservative felt secure with "her cash on hand" because she knew that the bank had walls made of thick concrete with steel reinforcements and the most modern of security systems and theft deterrents. In addition, the manager had ensured her that the bank had guards on duty 24 hours a day, 365 days a year. What could possibly cause her to lose money in the carefully thought out plan?

First, money sitting in a safe deposit box does not earn interest. This woman did not make any money on her money. Secondly, she failed to realize that inflation was slowly but surely drying up her money stream. Even such a conservative approach cannot escape all possible risk!

What you can and must do is emulate the Union and Confederate generals at Gettysburg. Both Robert E. Lee and George Meade had carefully constructed battle plans, which they hoped would minimize the risk of causalities to their troops. The generals had to consider topography, artillery positioning, supply lines, and picket placements. Today's investor must consider market risk in the event that the financial market performs poorly. They must also beware of business risk that would lower the value of a particular stock because of poor performance of the issuing company. Furthermore, there is the interest-rate risk. As you recall from Chapter Seven, interest rates have a direct impact upon the market. When interest rates rise, stocks do not usually perform well and the value of bonds decrease. And finally, let's not forget the silent enemy of inflation. Very conservative investors may go broke slowly because inflation decreases their future purchasing power.

The troops at Gettysburg could not avoid all of the risks of battle; they had to focus on those risks they could not eliminate and determine strategies for minimizing their impact. Likewise, you as the investor must be aware of the risks you face and develop strategies for managing those risks. In this chapter, I will give you several such strategies that you can put into place immediately.

Strategy #1 is called dollar cost averaging. To implement this strategy, the investor contributes a specific amount of money each month into a stock or mutual fund. When the value of the stock/mutual fund increases, the investor will receive fewer shares. When the value decreases, the investor can buy more shares for the same amount of money. Historically, letting such investments "ride" and consistently investing the same amount every month, averaging the share price over a typical market cycle, produces a better long-term gain than moving money in and out of investments. The graph on the following page depicts how dollar cost averaging works.

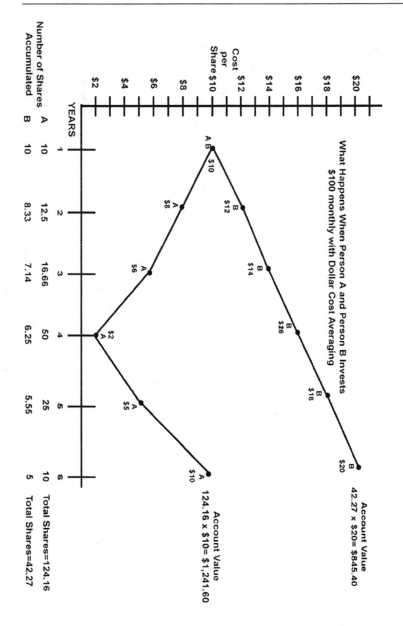

What Happens When Person A and Person B Invests
$100 monthly with Dollar Cost Averaging

Strategy #2 is referred to as staggering fixed-income maturities. Following this strategy, the investor staggers the maturity dates of her/his bond investments as a technique to manage volatility of the interest-rate risk. This enables the investor to hold all securities until their specified maturity date and to reinvest his/her money at staggered times at varying interest rates.

Strategy #3 is known as asset allocation. Just as General Lee did not put all of his artillery pieces on the same Gettysburg ridge, and General Meade did not march all of his divisions down the same road into the same line of battle, you should not put all your investment money in one place. There are some basic guidelines to assist in determining your appropriate asset allocation. One is your time horizon: the more time you have until retirement, the greater the risk you can comfortably handle. Secondly, examine your objectives for investing and be honest with yourself about your risk tolerance.

The generals practiced a form of asset allocation by conducting skirmishes on several fronts within the battle as a whole. So, too, investors can hedge against inflation and business risks by diversifying their holdings. Simply stated, the definition of asset allocation is *don't put all of your eggs in one basket.*

Many people will say they are aggressive until they see the value of their account drop; then they become conservative. This can be very damaging to your portfolio because it allows two emotions into your portfolio that have no business being there. The first is FEAR, and the other is GREED. In the late '90s, many people entered the market very late in the game because everyone else was making money and they wanted a piece of the action. Then in 2002, people became fearful of a downturn and there was a tremendous sell-off. Investors in these situations were acting upon fear and greed. A proper asset allocation can help you to mitigate the downside while capturing the upside, but you must not allow those two emotions to dictate your investing decisions.

Ask yourself, "Can I control:

- **the stock market**

- **asset allocation**

- **contributions and withdrawals**

If you answered "yes" to #1, please call me right away. I'd love to be able to provide a guaranteed return to my clients! You do have some control over #2 and #3, however. Concentrate on these two elements to control investment risks, and you can keep your financial stream healthy and flowing. The major point is that investing is not just about finding the best stock or bond but also that you save in a consistent, systematic, and organized manner.

LIFE RISKS

It is equally important to examine your life risks and develop a strategy to protect yourself from these risks. On the battlefield, a general may find that his troops are not properly positioned to win the battle. The general can manage this risk in one of four ways:

He can choose to do nothing, in which case, he carries the full weight of risk directly on his shoulders and will probably lose the fight. He may choose not to fight at all. Then he avoids participating in a risk-creating activity. He also may move only a few troops to a more advantageous position and reduce the risk. Finally, he may ask his other commanding officers to move the troops where they think the troops should be, thus transferring the risk.

The retiree can use a variety of insurance options to manage his/her life risks in much the same way.

Retirees may elect to be fully accountable for any risk and sustain the entire financial hardship that may be associated with such actions, or they may attempt to reduce or avoid the risk altogether. An example would be with any health-related issues or activities. Finally, they may elect to transfer any known or unforeseen risk by purchasing insurance coverage for health and/or property.

Naturally, the higher the risk, the more likely that it may be detrimental to your financial welfare. Therefore, every effort should be made to transfer the risk before it can have a crippling effect.

I am a licensed life and health insurance agent, but in this book I will not provide you with specific advice on purchasing any form of insurance. I do strongly recommend that you discuss your life risks with a reputable agent to determine which, if any, insurance purchases are right for you. If you already have policies, carefully review the conditions and terms of your policies to ensure that their values match your risk needs. Here are some examples of important coverage to look for:

Home Owner's Insurance – Look for a clause that covers loss at replacement value, rather than purchase/market price. Remember that your house and its contents may well have appreciated, increasing the value beyond your actual purchase price.

Auto Insurance – Many policy holders have coverage that provides up to $50,000 per person and $100,000 per incident. This may not be adequate protection.

Renter's Insurance – If you are renting a residence, you should have renter's insurance. The building owner's policy will not cover your personal possessions lost or damaged as a result of theft, vandalism, fire, smoke, or other disasters.

Umbrella Liability – You may want to consider a one-million-dollar umbrella, which would add additional coverage to your current home owner and auto coverage. An umbrella can also provide coverage for legal fees and liabilities not covered by other policies.

Health Insurance – For our purposes here, we will discuss only Medicare and Medicaid health coverage, since this is most relevant for retirees.

Medicare Part A is a federally sponsored health insurance policy that can provide coverage at the beginning of the month in which you turn 65. Once you are enrolled, Medicare will provide partial coverage for hospitalization and limited nursing home care.

Medicare Part B is optional. If you select Part B coverage, Medicare will cover a portion of your doctor's fees, most out-patient services, and other medically related services.

Medicare Part C enables those eligible for Medicare to choose either a traditional Medicare program or a Medicare + Choice plan, such as coordinated-care plans, private fee-for-service plans, and medical savings accounts.

Medicare Part D provides partial coverage for prescription drugs and prescribed deliverable medical equipment (wheelchair, oxygen, etc.).

Medicare won't pay for long-term nursing care. It is intended to provide coverage for short-term medical treatment that will restore the covered individual to full health. Medicare does cover some hospitalization, but because of its reimbursement structure, most hospitals now release Medicare patients as soon as they are stabilized. Medicare covers nursing home care if admission follows hospitalization of at least three days and only as long as the patient is improving.

According to the Department of Health and Human Services, in 2006 Medicare paid:

- **All eligible expenses for a nursing home stay for days 1-20**

- **Expenses over $114.00 per day for days 21-100**

- **Nothing for days 101 and beyond**

Here are some important things to consider concerning Medicare:

Ensure that you have made all the proper arrangements for Medicare coverage to begin when you turn 65. If you plan to retire before age 65, you may want to consider carrying health coverage with another provider until you are Medicare eligible.

- **Consider a Medicare supplement or a Medigap policy to cover expenses that will not be covered by Medicare.**

- **If you enroll in Medicare Part B after age 65 or if you enroll, drop out, and re-enroll, you may pay higher premiums.**

- **If you plan to travel internationally after you retire, you may want supplemental coverage. Medicare does not cover medical expenses incurred outside of the United States.**

- Check the Social Security Administration's Web site at www.ssa.gov or contact them toll free at 1-800-772-1213 for additional information.

Medicaid is the US health insurance program for individuals and families with low incomes and limited resources. It is jointly funded by the states and federal government, and is managed by the states. Among the groups of people served by Medicaid are eligible low-income parents, children, seniors, and people with disabilities. Medicaid is the largest source of funding for medical and health-related services for people with limited income. Below are some important facts regarding this program.

- **The patient must have spent all but $2,000 in countable assets. A spouse may retain assets, including the home.**

- **Some states set income limits or allow income equal to the cost of privately paid care or Medicare reimbursement care in the local area.**

- **Medicaid considers a "look-back period" when determining eligibility. Any assets transferred from the patient's ownership within 36-60 months prior to applying for Medicaid will be considered in determining eligibility. Intentionally transferring assets to qualify for Medicaid is a federal crime.**

Disability Income Protection – Once during a retirement seminar, I asked the participants to name their most valuable asset. One man, in the back of the room, put his arm around his wife and announced, "She is." While I applaud his romantic sentiment, one of your most important

85

assets during your working years is your ability to produce income. Don't make the mistake of assuming it is unlikely that you may become disabled prior to retirement. According to the *2005 Field Guide* from the National Underwriter, a 40-year-old man is three times more likely to become disabled than he is to die. At age 50, his risk of disability is two times more likely than death. Long-term disability income insurance will provide a percentage of your working income should you become disabled to the point of being unable to work. You may want to consider a policy that will provide 65-75 percent of your regular income.

Long-Term Care – Medicare was never intended to provide long-term care, and Medicaid, which may provide financial resources for some, should not be deemed appropriate for meeting your potential long-term needs. The following chart, from the Centers for Medicare and Medicaid Services, 2003, illustrates how most people pay for long-term care expenses. In 2006 the percentages were relatively the same.

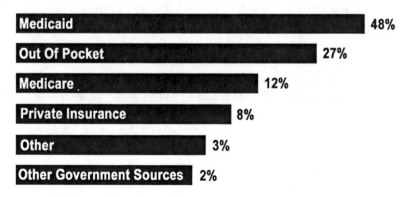

Medicaid 48%
Out Of Pocket 27%
Medicare 12%
Private Insurance 8%
Other 3%
Other Government Sources 2%

It is expected that the cost of nursing home care will escalate over the next 15 years. The data, which came from the 2005 Field Guide, assumes a 5% annual increase compounded annually. For example, the average monthly cost for nursing home care will rise from a current approximate rate of $4,667 to over $9,700 within 15 years.

Long-term care insurance enables the elderly to avoid dependency on others, helps protect their assets, provides additional resources for securing quality long-term care, protects them from the need for welfare and Medicaid, and helps them control options for future care. Long-term care coverage should be purchased only after considering all of your options. The contracts can be confusing, so please seek the advice of a professional.

Life Insurance – The amount of life insurance that is appropriate for you will change over the years as your life situations change. Typically, an individual needs a larger policy when he/she still has minor dependents, a high mortgage, considerable debt, and the need for educational funding. As you age, you may find that your needs change, and I strongly suggest that you review your life insurance needs and current policy with a professional periodically.

Before you go out and buy a policy, here is a simple way to figure out how much you need. Remember, there are very few reasons to buy more insurance than you really need. The only thing you will be doing is making the insurance company more money. And always seek a professional before purchasing any policy.

Sample Life Insurance Needs Analysis

Survivor Income Needs (annually)	$ 50,000
Lump sum needed to produce income (assuming a 5% rate of withdrawal)	$1,000,000
Debt and tuition cost for 2 minor children	$ 500,000
Burial and estate settling costs	$ 30,000
Subtotal	$1,530,000
Current assets (i.e. 401k, mutual fund, etc…)	($ 500,000)
Current life insurance	($ 250,000)
Total additional life insurance needed	$ 780,000

We all know how life insurance works. You pay a premium based on the amount of coverage you need. Premium costs may change depending upon gender, age, health of the insured, and the type of policy you purchase.

Basically there are two types of life insurance: term and cash value, such as whole life or universal life. Term life provides a death benefit only for a specific period or the term of the policy. If you die during the term of the policy, your beneficiary receives the death benefit, tax-free. If you live beyond the term of the policy, there is no benefit. Cash value life insurance pays a death benefit to your survivor while the policy is in force. If you live beyond the specified period, you will have accumulated cash value, which will be available to you. Check with your insurance company to find out the specific rules when withdrawing funds from your policies.

The moral for the modern investor is to focus on those elements over which you do have control and don't worry about what the market does from day to day. Failure to implement sound strategies for managing investment risks may have you sounding like Pickett responding to General Lee: "Sir, I have no retirement funds!"

CHAPTER 9
DEVELOPING YOUR EXIT STRATEGY: ESTATE PLANNING

"The cost of living is going up, and the chance of living is going down."

FLIP WILSON

Tom Carhart, in his book, *Lost Triumph: Lee's Real Plan at Gettysburg—And Why It Failed*, discusses General Lee's battle plan for day #3 at Gettysburg, which he believed was different from what actually occurred. Carhart's theory was that Pickett's Charge was supposed to have been the frontal assault of a planned pincer movement. If this plan had worked, Lee may have changed the outcome of Gettysburg and possibly the Civil War itself. This plan may have been upset by General George Custer, whose troops, although outnumbered, fought aggressively and saved the day for the Union.

General Lee's strategy should have had all of his troops in appropriate locations throughout the Gettysburg battlefield. You, too, need to insure that you have a strategy in place that will appropriately allocate your assets after your death. This strategy is known as estate planning. Just as the privates at Gettysburg gave little thought to the strategy of troop movements, so many of us tend to think that estate planning is just for the very wealthy and therefore of no real concern to us. Take a minute and add up all your assets, including life insurance and retirement plan benefits. You may well find that your estate is quite large. So here's the plan.

Before you start anything, I would strongly suggest that you contact a competent attorney. Estate planning can be very complex, and you want to make sure it is done correctly.

During your estate planning, you should first start by planning for your incapacity. While we all are going to die one day, there is also a good chance we may become unable to make financial and medical decisions during our life. The three main documents that you will need are a Durable Power of Attorney, a Health-Care Advance Directive, and a Living Will.

DURABLE POWER OF ATTORNEY

This document is also called a Power of Attorney for Financial Matters, and it designates the individual whom you authorize to make financial decisions on your behalf if you are unable to do so. Sometimes it takes effect immediately, without regard to an individual's incapacity. Some couples choose this method because frequent traveling makes it difficult for one spouse to tend to his or her financial affairs while abroad. In most cases, though, the document "springs into effect" if you are mentally or physically incapacitated, and ceases to work once you are no longer incapacitated. This type is known as a "Springing Power of Attorney" for that reason. It also should specify the process of determining at what point you are considered unable to manage your affairs. Even if you are the beneficiary on the account, you will still need this document if the person is still living and unable to make financial decisions.

HEALTH-CARE ADVANCE DIRECTIVE

This document is also called a Power of Attorney for Health Care, and it designates the individual whom you authorize to make medical decisions on your behalf if you are mentally or physically incapacitated or simply unable to communicate your wishes because you are under anesthesia. A well-drafted health-care advance directive will include language complying with the Health Insurance Portability and Accountability Act of 1996, 42 USC 1320d ("HIPAA") so that your health-care providers will be able to share information with your designee without fear of legal ramifications over privacy issues. It will also give end-of-life decision-making authority to your designee, including the power to withdraw treatment, which in many states would replace or supersede a living will. These forms are available at most hospitals, or you may have one drafted by your attorney.

LIVING WILL

This document is sometimes called a Declaration, and it instructs the hospital of your wishes if your physicians have determined that your death will occur and where life-sustaining procedures would serve only to artificially prolong the dying process. In a living will, you have the power to direct that such procedures be withheld or withdrawn, and that you be permitted to die naturally with only the administration of medication or the performance of any medical procedure deemed necessary to provide you with comfort or care or to alleviate pain. On the other hand, you could choose to authorize every extraordinary measure available to keep you alive, if that was your wish.

It is also possible to indicate your preference for or against organ and tissue donation in a living will. Again, there are forms available from most hospitals or from your attorney.

Now that you have planned for your incapacity, you can now plan for your death. A good estate plan will provide the following:

- **Instructions regarding the physical and financial care of your family members, including the appointment of guardians for your minor children**

- **Distributing your assets to individuals and institutions according to your wishes**

- **Reducing the cost of settling your estate**

- **Minimizing taxes**

Without proper estate planning, a court will decide who will administer your estate and care for your minor children. The court will ensure that all children are treated equally, even though they may have very different needs. A conservator will be court-appointed to oversee the money left to minor children, and the children will receive the assets at age 18. The court may determine that distant relatives should receive assets that you would have preferred left to close friends. And your estate may pay unnecessary taxes and expenses, diminishing the amount available for your heirs.

In addition to your stated preference in the will, which we will talk about soon, your assets are distributed to beneficiaries through one of four means: direct transfer, joint ownership, trusts, and probate. Usually the goal is to have as much of the assets transfer to your heirs without going through probate in order to reduce the time, expense, and hassle that loved ones would otherwise have to endure in the process of closing your estate.

DIRECT TRANSFER

This occurs when your asset has a payable-upon-death clause or a beneficiary designation. A certified copy of your death certificate is all that is required to transfer ownership. Savings accounts and certificates of deposit fall into this category. Many states also have provisions to include stocks and mutual fund accounts to be registered as "transfer-on-death" accounts. Similarly, 401(k)s, 403(b)s, IRAs, Roth IRAs, tax-deferred annuities, and life insurance benefits can be transferred in a short time with minimal effort to the designated beneficiaries.

Assets transferred this way would avoid probate, but that also could be a problem. Let's say you never looked at your beneficiary forms on your 401(k), but you made sure your will left everything to your son. Then you pass away, and when the son goes to get your 401(k) the company informs him that he is not the beneficiary. Unfortunately, you left your former girlfriend's name on as primary beneficiary. Guess who gets all the money? THE GIRLFRIEND! Be careful to always keep copies and review your beneficiary forms after any life-changing event.

JOINT OWNERSHIP

This is a common method that enables two or more people to own a particular asset, such as a car, a house, or property. Let's say Mary and John are married and own a house, which is titled in joint ownership. John passes away. Mary inherits John's share of the house as well as having her own share. For tax purposes, all or a portion of the asset may be included in the estate of the deceased. Tenants in Common is similar to joint ownership but generally involves two or more individuals who are not married and may or may not be related. Just in case you live in one of the nine Community Property states, remember that property acquired during the marriage is owned equally by the husband and wife, regardless of how the deed is written.

TRUSTS

A trust is a legal document that is used to control the management and transfer of specific assets. There are four basic types of trusts, which have definitive purposes.

A **Testamentary Trust** is set up inside of your Last Will & Testament, and is funded upon your death. In this way, you own and control the assets of the trust until your death, and you may set the conditions under which beneficiaries receive the trust's assets. Additionally, a testamentary trust can be used to reduce or defer estate taxes.

A **Living Trust** takes effect during your lifetime and provides lifetime financial management, transfers assets upon your death, and avoids probate.

A **Revocable Trust** gives the owner the right to change the terms and conditions of the trust and to avoid probate. Be aware, however, that asset protection, tax savings, and estate-tax savings may not apply if the owner has the right to control the trust.

Let me spend a moment on the revocable trust. Many

people put their children on as joint owners of their homes. Why? Because at their death, the home will avoid probate and pass directly to the child. This approach makes sense from a transfer standpoint, but it can be devastating when it comes to taxes. Let's say Mom bought the house for $50,000 (her cost basis) 20 years ago, and the day she died it was worth $200,000. If she had left it to the child in her will then the cost basis would have received a step-up. Basically that means when the child who inherited the home goes to sell it, the IRS is not going to tax them on the $150,000 gain. Why? Because the market value of that home the day she died ($200,000) became the new cost basis. So if Mom had put the child on as joint owner during her lifetime, she would have also gifted half the cost basis. In this scenario, half of the house would get a step-up in cost basis, and the other half would not. When the child went to sell it, half of the house would subject the child to capital gains taxes and half would not.

Now what would be an easy solution? Mom could have re-titled the house during her lifetime into a **Revocable Living Trust** and made the child the beneficiary. Then when she passed away, the home would get a step-up in cost basis, avoid probate, and be distributed directly to the child via the trust.

An **Irrevocable Trust** – There are two common forms of the irrevocable trust, which cannot be cancelled or changed. The first is the **Charitable Remainder Trust**, which allows you to give assets to a charity while receiving an income from the trust while you are still living. Upon your death, the charity receives the value of the trust. If the charity sells the assets of the trust, capital gains taxes are avoided. The value of the trust is usually excluded from the value of your estate, and a charitable income tax deduction is available. The second type of irrevocable trust is the **Irrevocable Life Insurance Trust**. This trust is usually structured to hold and manage life insurance policies and, sometimes, other assets. This trust is often referred to as an "ILIT" and simply means that although you are still the insured under your life insurance policy, the policy itself is actually owned by the trust, which has its own tax ID number. Because you are not the owner, the death benefit paid to the trust at your death is not part of your taxable estate. In this way, this trust passes the death benefits to the trust's beneficiaries free of estate tax. However, be aware that property given to the trust may be subject to the gift tax and/or require the filing of an informational gift tax return.

PROBATE

Assets that are not passed on through direct transfer, joint ownership, or trusts may be transferred under the supervision of the court by means of a legal process that identifies what you own at the time of your death and distributes those assets according to your wishes or state law. One thing to remember is that everything that passes through probate becomes public record and can incur additional cost.

Here is the process of probate:

- **Establishes whether a will exists**
- **Appoints an executor or personal representative**
- **Values your entire estate**
- **Receives and pays taxes and claims against your estate**
- **Settles disputes**

- **Distributes your assets to appropriate beneficiaries**

Now let's talk about the characteristics of a **will**. A will is a legal document that takes effect at your death. A proper will can accomplish some of the following things:

- **Indicate whom you want to receive your assets (those that were not transferred by other means)**
- **Name the personal representative or executor whom you want to handle your estate**
- **Control how the assets are distributed**
- **Indicate how you would like to care for any minor children**
- **Take advantage of any estate-tax saving strategies**

TAXES

There are three types of taxes involved in settling an estate: **income taxes, state inheritance taxes,** and **federal estate taxes.** If you didn't already know, you can't escape the tax man even when you are dead! After you die, your estate will owe tax on any income earned during the year in which you passed, as well as income that your estate earns between death and the time the estate is distributed, and finally, on the untaxed portion of your IRAs, tax-deferred annuities, and retirement plans. The lone exception is if your spouse is the beneficiary and chooses to roll the money over into his/her own IRA or other qualified plan (note: there are other strategies to potentially defer taxes to non-spouse beneficiaries). There is a federal gift and estate tax on assets you transfer to others. In 2006 annual gifts of $12,000 and gifts to charities and your spouse are exempt. Each person also has a lifetime gift exclusion limit of $1,000,000.

As for your estate, the current exclusion amount that can transfer free of the federal estate tax at your death is $2,000,000. In 2009, this exclusion increases to $3,500,000. However, federal estate taxes are scheduled to be repealed in 2010, and the law repealing them "sunsets" at the end of December, 2010. Basically anything over $2,000,000 in your taxable estate at your death will be taxed at a maximum rate of 46%. The rate will drop to 45% in 2007 to 2009, and in 2010 there are no federal estate taxes. The problem is in 2011 when the rate goes back to 55%. This tax can drastically reduce what you leave to your heirs.

You should also be mindful that many states also have their own "Inheritance Tax," which can be set at a lower benchmark than the federal estate tax. At one time, many states tied their inheritance tax to the current federal estate tax exclusion amount, so that if your estate was not subject to federal estate tax, it was also exempt from any state inheritance taxes. However, because that exclusion has risen considerably in recent years, some states have deliberately "decoupled" their own inheritance tax rate from the federal estate tax exclusion, as a way to raise revenue. This uncertainty makes it important to consult with an estate-planning attorney to make certain that changes in both federal and state law are factored into your plan.

You can estimate your estate's tax liability by taking your gross estate minus your debts, burial costs, and fees, and costs of settling your estate equals your adjusted taxable estate.

What is your **gross estate**? It is everything you own or control at the time of your death, including assets in your own name, your share of joint assets, IRA and retirement plan balances, survivor income benefits on policies you own, life insurance benefits, debts you own, and annuity death benefits.

Your **Adjusted Gross Estate** is your gross estate minus debts, burial costs, and fees and costs of settling your estate. And your **Taxable Estate** is your adjusted gross estate minus amounts left to charities and amounts left to your spouse.

Before we finish this chapter, I have to stress again that I strongly recommend that you meet with a competent estate-planning attorney when formulating, establishing, and executing your estate plan. I am not an attorney, and none of the above information can be used as legal advice. It is only used as a means of providing a basic understanding of estate planning.

Like life insurance, you should review your will periodically and make any necessary changes. A good rule of thumb is to review your will and your beneficiary designations on other assets when you move to a new state, your marital status changes, your youngest child turns 18, you want to change a beneficiary or an allocation, when there is a significant change in the value of your estate, or when Congress changes laws that might affect your estate.

The generals at Gettysburg did not make one definitive battle plan and stick to it. As skirmishes occurred on various parts of the battlefield, they reviewed and revised their strategies. You can earn your general's stars if you periodically review your estate-planning strategy and ensure that it is still your best battle plan. Here's a "voice" to illustrate this important point.

Mr. & Mrs. John Doe were married for 20 years. Mary Doe was listed as the sole beneficiary on her husband's $100,000 life insurance policy as well as on his

retirement accounts. The couple divorced and Mr. Doe remarried. At the time of his death, he had three small children with his second wife. Imagine the surprise and consternation of Mrs. Doe II when she discovered that her husband had not thought to change his beneficiary after his divorce. In most cases Mrs. Doe I inherits, and the second wife and children are left penniless.

CHAPTER 10
KNOWING WHEN TO CALL IN THE CAVALRY:
HIRING PROFESSIONALS

"In the morning, there's to be a great battle. Tomorrow or the next day will determine the war."

GENERAL ROBERT E. LEE

Geneva Lee sent orders to his cavalry commander, Jeb Stuart, prior to the Gettysburg campaign, and those orders have since become a source of controversy among those who interpret them. One theory is that the orders were giving Stuart leave to ride around the Federal army. Others believe Lee's intention was that the cavalry screen and scout ahead of the army as it advanced into Maryland and Pennsylvania.

Correspondence, Orders, And Returns Relating to Operations In North Carolina, Virginia, West Virginia, Maryland, Pennsylvania, And Department of the East, from June 3 To August 3, 1863. Confederate Correspondence. Etc. - #1
O.R. - SERIES I - VOLUME XXVII/3 [S# 45]

Headquarters Army of Northern Virginia
June 23, 1863--5 p.m.

Maj. Gen. J. E. B. STUART,
Commanding Cavalry:

General,

Your notes of 9 and 10.30 a.m. to-day have just been received. As regards the purchase of tobacco for your men, supposing that Confederate money will not be taken, I am willing for your commissaries or quartermasters to purchase this tobacco and let the men get it from them, but I can have nothing seized by the men.

If General Hooker's army remains inactive, you can leave two brigades to watch him, and withdraw with the three others, but should he not appear to be moving northward, I think you had better withdraw this side of the mountain to-morrow night, cross at Shepherdstown next day, and move over to Fredericktown.

You will, however, be able to judge whether you can pass around their army without hindrance, doing them all the damage you can, and cross the river east of the mountains. In either case, after crossing the river, you must move on and feel the right of Ewell's troops, collecting information, provisions, &c.

Give instructions to the commander of the brigades left behind, to watch the flank and rear of the army, and (in the event of the enemy leaving their front) retire from the mountains west of the Shenandoah, leaving sufficient pickets to guard the passes, and bringing everything clean along the Valley, closing upon the rear of the army.

As regards the movements of the two brigades of the enemy moving toward Warrenton, the commander of the brigades to be left in the mountains must do what he can to counteract them, but I think the sooner you cross into Maryland, after to-morrow, the better.

The movements of Ewell's corps are as stated in my former

letter. Hill's first division will reach the Potomac to-day, and Longstreet will follow to-morrow.

Be watchful and circumspect in all your movements.

I am, very respectfully and truly, yours
R. E. Lee
General.

Both Union and Confederate generals considered their cavalry troops to be the army's "eyes and ears." The mounted cavalry could move farther and faster than the infantry. Their main function was to keep the generals informed of enemy troop movements and locations.

In the first nine chapters of this book, you have read numerous strategies to win each skirmish on the retirement battlefield. It is important to know that a skirmish is won having enough weapons, correct troop placements, and adequate funding for soldiers' pay and provisions. More importantly, the battle is won through a comprehensive approach.

Just as the generals needed their cavalry, you, too, need the support of your own "cavalry" comprised of experienced professionals, and you must know when to ask for their guidance. You can ask many questions, like "How much life insurance do I need?" but you must remember that every financial decision made in isolation impacts all aspects of your financial well-being. Like the generals, reflect on the retirement battlefield as a whole, staying focused on your goals. The correct answers are within you, the individual. This book simply serves as a foundation. Think of this planning in terms of building a house. First you must lay a strong foundation, but you don't live in the foundation. You need to correctly implement your financial decisions to actually build a sturdy financial house.

In summary, here's a step-by-step planning process:

- You cannot procrastinate. Yesterday is history, tomorrow is a mystery, and today is a gift. That's why it is called the present. Make a gift to yourself by making today "decision day." Define what retirement means to you and set your retirement goals.

- Next, determine where you are right now in terms of your cash flow, budget, debts, and savings. Where is all your money going? I can't emphasize enough how important a budget is in winning the retirement battle. If you combine your current budget with your retirement goals, you can come up with a realistic estimate of your monthly and annual retirement expenses. Make certain that your savings plan is consistent. Haphazard savings practices will lead to defeat. You may also find it helpful to set up inventory and cash flow statements.

- Now find a good financial planner or advisor. The title may vary from area to area, so don't select this important member of your cavalry based solely on title. Interview a number of planners. Ask questions like "How are you paid?" There is really no right or wrong answer, but you need to know and understand this payment process. Financial planners usually set charges that are either commission based, fee based, or a combination of the two. Ask if they do comprehensive financial planning for clients. If so, ask for their definition of a comprehensive financial plan. By now you should have gained some insight from this book as to what is an appropriate response. You will want to know if the planner is a Registered Investment Advisor. You can verify the response by asking to see a copy of her/his Form

ADV, Part II. This form is a required disclosure document to be offered to clients and potential clients to help them evaluate the qualifications of a Registered Investment Advisor. You will want to know how long the planner has been in the business and what certifications they have earned. It takes a great deal of time and commitment to earn certain certifications, so having one speaks well of their dedication to the profession. And finally, you may want to know if the firm you are considering has a succession plan. You need to know what will happen if the individual you are dealing with dies or retires. In 2001 when my firm, Kissinger Financial Services, Inc. merged with Sanders Morris Harris, Inc., they viewed my father's position as the firm's sole financial planner as both an asset and a liability. As long as my dad was able to produce, he was an asset. If he couldn't due to some unforeseen occurrence, he would then be considered a liability. Before the merger was approved, Sanders Harris Morris wanted a comprehensive succession plan and recruited me from Merrill Lynch to join my dad as his vice president.

- When you have all these answers, you can decide who will be a viable financial planner for you. Think of your financial planner as your battlefield general. That individual will help to coordinate all your financial services needs and communicate with the other members of your "cavalry": your estate-planning attorney, your CPA, and your insurance agent. If you selected wisely, your "general" will know how to execute an excellent financial plan. But remember, YOU are the commander-in-chief. The "general" and the cavalry can make suggestions and provide guidance, but in the end you are responsible for winning the battle.

CHAPTER 11
THE COST OF LOSING THE BATTLE

"Bankruptcy is a legal proceeding in which you put your money in your pants pocket and give your coat to your creditors."

JOEY ADAMS

On July 2nd, Union Major General Dan Sickles made a conscious decision to ignore the orders he had been given to place his troops along Cemetery Ridge. Sickles felt this position on the low ground to be difficult to defend and chose, instead, to position his Third Corps on the boulder-covered heights of Devil's Den. They were stretched along the southern end of a wheat field, through a peach orchard, and then bending back to follow north along the Emmitsburg Road. Sickles' unauthorized move had provided him with a more defensible position, but left a gap between his troops and the rest of the Union line. The Confederacy exploited this gap with a series of bloody skirmishes, resulting in hundreds of casualties for the Union army. Equally important, Sickles' unapproved move left Little Round Top, Big Round Top, and the Union left flank completely undefended. When General George Meade learned of what Sickles had done, he was furious and ordered Sickles back to his original position. Sickles could no longer comply with his commander's order, even if he wanted. A 12-pound cannonball tore through his right leg, nearly severing it. To some degree, Sickles left his military career in "bankruptcy." A leg and a career were a high price to pay for taking an unauthorized risk!

As I have mentioned frequently throughout this book, listen to the strategies of the commanding generals of Gettysburg, Meade and Lee, by assembling a corps of your own qualified experts to assist in planning your retirement strategies. If you elect to enter the battle alone, you may find yourself in Sickles' peach orchard, engaged in a financial battle you cannot win. And you, too, may have to pay a high price for the cost of losing your retirement battle ~ forfeiting a comfortable and secure income for the rest of your life.

Unlike this book, don't let your financial welfare end in Chapter 11.

EPILOGUE

Abraham Lincoln once said, "Nearly all men can stand adversity, but if you want to test a man's character...give him power."

Ned Kissinger has grown to be a leader in the field of financial services, and whether he knows it or not, he has obtained the power Mr. Lincoln was talking about. Ned would never tell you he feels that way about himself because he is too humble. Remember his story in the prologue about the elderly lady in the Gettysburg Diner? I can tell you he has a heart for business because he has a heart for people. I know this not only because I am his father, but because I have had the pleasure and privilege of working side by side with Ned for the last six years.

From his youth, Ned had a good sense of value, and by the age of 11 he became active in the stock market. My wife, Debbie, and I instilled a sense of goal setting in our children and financially matched any savings they would invest. That foundation grew in Ned a sense of good, sound financial practices, and by the age of 21, Ned had built a substantial account with which to begin his adult life and career.

We always had a rule that a father can't hire his child. When I decided to merge Kissinger Financial Services in 2001, I was no longer the employer. At the time, Ned was employed with Merrill Lynch, and he elected to go down to Houston, which is where our new parent company, SMH Capital Inc., was located. They had strict hiring standards, and Ned had to earn the right to come here.

He has been an incredible business asset. He has helped

revolutionize and transition us from the old-fashioned commission-based business. I can say with professional confidence, this young man knows what he is talking about!

Ned is a born leader and has earned a great deal of industry respect thus far during his career. Although I am his father, I tell you with great sincerity that I have learned more from him than he has ever learned from me.

Having tapped into Ned's talents by reading this book, I have no doubt he has made the retirement planning process for you a more understandable part of your life. Best wishes for a bright and prosperous future,

Bill
William I. Kissinger, CPA/PFS, CFP®, ChFEBC
President, Kissinger Financial Services, Inc

RESOURCES

Note: URLs are tested before publication, but their access is not guaranteed after publication. Most sources can be referenced by the reader through printing publications if needed.

Web Story References
Chapter 2
http://americanhistory.about.com/library/weekly/aa101601a.htm
Chapter 3
http://www.csasilverdollar.com/longstreet.html
Chapter 4
http://www.jennie-wade-house.com/
Chapter 5
http://www.civilwarhome.com/Pay.htm
Chapter 6
http://business.centurytel.net/2ndwivi-coa/ag.html
Chapter 7
http://www.financialhistory.org/fh/2000/evening.htm
Chapter 8
http://www.americancivilwar.com/getty.html
Chapter 9
http://www.riderinfo.com/motorcycle-books/isbn0399152490.html
Chapter 10
http://ehistory.osu.edu/uscw/library/or/045/0923.cfm
Chapter 11
http://www.brotherswar.com/Gettysburg-2h.htm

Web References-General
American Stock Exchange
http://www.amex.com/
Center for Disease Control and Prevention
http://www.cdc.gov/nchs/agingact.htm

Department of Health and Human Services
http://www.hhs.gov/
Federal Deposit Insurance Corporation
http://www.fdic.gov/

Journal of Studies on Alcohol and Drugs
http://www.jsad.com/jsad/article/Alcohol_Consumption_by_Elderly_Americans/1138.ht
ml
Historical Inflation Rates
http://inflationdata.com/Inflation/Inflation_Rate/HistoricalInflation.aspx
Internal Revenue Service
http://www.irs.gov/
NASDAQ Stock Exchange
http://www.nasdaq.com/
New York Securities Exchange
http://www.nyse.com/
Social Security Administration
http://www.ssa.gov/
Retirement Savings Planner
http://www.torrid-tech.com/

Written References-General
Financial Strategies for Successful Retirement®
Copyright ©2005, SMMS, Inc.
Retirement Planning Today ™
FMT Solutions, Inc.
2005 Field Guide to Financial Planning
By Donald F. Cady

CREDITS

Editors: Eric Seaborg and Maggie Kiewitt have over forty years of experience in all aspects of human resources management, organizational development, and organizational logistics and operations. As Eric and Maggie steadily climbed the career ladder, they each occupied a variety of positions at all levels of management and leadership in locations throughout the east coast.

They have discovered a true chemistry for working together and for inspiring leadership and teamwork in others and have collaborated to form *Aspect Associates, LLC* a consulting firm located in Baltimore, Maryland specializing in human resources management and organizational development. They subscribe to a collaborative and interactive relationship with their clients through an energizing style they label "Edu-tainment"...injecting entertainment into education.

Their first book, *Eggs of Wisdom from the Easter Bunny* was written as a tool for mentoring new leaders within the business field. **Aspects Associates** also offers an entertaining and educational leadership seminar based on the book.

If you are interested in learning more about *Aspects Associates, LLC*, the authors, or Freddy the rabbit, check out their Web site at **www.aspectassociates.com**.

Cover Design: Craig Kirby is a senior design professional with the ability to implement design and market strategies that are creative, on budget, and well planned. He is the founder of *Visually Speaking,* an award-winning graphic design solutions firm for a wide range of marketing and business objectives serving the Baltimore-Washington corridor. Craig can be reached by email at **craig@visuallygraphic.com**.